I0058349

made it in
China

Graham Jeal
Simon Cann

mii
Publishing

Published by MII Publishing
33 Melrose Gardens
New Malden
Surrey KT3 3HQ
United Kingdom
www.madeitin.com

Copyright © Graham Jeal, Simon Cann 2009

All rights reserved. No part of this publication may be
reproduced in any form or by any means without the prior
permission of the publisher.

The information supplied by the featured entrepreneurs
has been reproduced in good-faith and after review by each
of the individuals. While every effort has been taken to
ensure accuracy, the authors and the publisher make no
representations about the accuracy of the information
contained in this book and cannot accept responsibility
for any errors or omissions, or for any loss based on the
content of this book. Where links to websites have been
included, these are offered as a resource for readers. No
warranty is given about the information or products
that may be available from any of these websites and no
endorsement is made of any site listed in this book.

This book mentions several brand names—these are all
the trademark of their respective owners. The featured
entrepreneurs occasionally mention certain individuals—
in limited circumstances, the names of some business
contacts have been changed.

Flag on cover: © Wmj82 | Dreamstime.com

ISBN 978-0-9561177-0-0

1.020081215

In memory of

Frank Trevett

and

Frances Jeal

whose inspiration is still felt today

Acknowledgements

We would like to thank everyone involved in the production of this book.

In particular we would like to thank the featured entrepreneurs: Scott Barrack, Bob Boyce, J C Lim, Grace Liu, Richard Robinson, Montgomery Singman, Paul Stepanek, and Henry Winter. These individuals have all generously taken the time to share their insights and understandings learned while doing business in China.

Each of the entrepreneurs would like to thank their Chinese colleagues, clients, customers, business partners, advisors, officials, and everyone who has helped them build their businesses and learn the lessons of doing business in China.

In addition we would like to extend our thanks to the following people who offered their comments about the current status of the Chinese investor market: Chris Rynning, Olivier Glauser, Adrian Li, and Rob McCormack.

About the Authors

Simon Cann

Simon Cann is the author of a number of business and music-related books including Rocking Your Music Business: Running Your Music Business at Home and on the Road, Becoming a Synthesizer Wizard: From Presets to Power User, How To Make A Noise, Cakewalk Synthesizers: From Presets to Power User, and Tolley's Basic Guide to Pensions (co-author). He has also had a behind-the-scenes role in many other publications.

Before turning his attention to full-time writing he spent over 15 years as a management consultant where his clients included global music industry, entertainment, and broadcasting companies, as well as companies in the financial services, aeronautical, pharmaceutical, and chemical industries.

You can read more about Simon and his writing at his website: simoncann.com.

Graham Jeal

Graham Jeal is a British born entrepreneur who has been working in China since 2001.

In 2002 Graham established Shanghai Vision Ltd, a property investment company which now has over 500 property investors from around the world and over US $200 million of assets under management.

Graham also set up Euro China Consulting Ltd, a consortium of companies spanning investment, venture capital, international trade, e-commerce, and the construction industry.

In 2007/2008 Graham was the President of the Entrepreneur Organization in China. He is a regular speaker at business forums in China and commentator on subjects involving business in China.

Previously Graham worked for JPMorgan in the City of London, New York, and Hong Kong. Graham lives in Shanghai.

About the *Made It In...* Series

The *Made It In...* series of books feature the personal experiences and lessons of international entrepreneurs who have built successful companies in the hottest business locations around the world.

The books feature successful entrepreneurs who have:

- left their own country and built businesses in other countries where cultures and business practices differ

- invested their own money—no one has been featured who works for someone else, and

- succeeded.

Each book focuses on the practical experiences of these individuals as they grew their companies in these new and developing markets. Their stories are both practical and entertaining, combining first-hand anecdotes about the challenges they faced and how these were met with their own observations and thoughts for dealing with each situation. Their stories are authenticated by their success.

For further information about the *Made It In...* series of books, including forthcoming titles, check out the website: madeitin.com.

If you want to know when the next publication in the series is available, then please join the mailing list (by clicking the Mailing List button at madeitin.com). Your email address will only be used to tell you about any future *Made It In...* publications and will not be shared.

Table of Contents

Foreword 1

Introduction
Welcome to China: Understanding China 3
Coming to China 4
Trying to Understand China 5
   Dynastic China: the Communist Dynasty 6
   You Will Never Be Chinese 7
   China Works 7
The Legal Framework 8
   The Role of the Notary Public 9
   Chinese Contracts Are Written In Poetry 9
   Apparent Disregard for Contract Law 10
   Intellectual Property 10
If You're Going to China... Then Go 11

Chapter 1
Manufacturing in China 13
Getting to China 14
Communism and the Cultural Revolution 17
   Guanxi-ocracy 18
   ...to Meritocracy... 19
   ...to an Upside-Down Society 19
How to Manufacture in China 21
   Setting Up Your Own Factory 21
   Contract Manufacturing 22
   Chinafy the Process 22
Managing Growth in Times of Chaos 23
When the Price Is Too Good 25
   How the Quotation Process Works 25
   The Chinese Approach to Contracts 27
   Management by Walking Around 28
   Getting a Proper Quote and the Devil 28
   Getting What You Order 30
   Who is to Blame When It Goes Wrong? 31

Moving From Manufacturing to Innovation....33
   Artisan Class......................................34
   Moving Up the Value Chain: Westerners Giving Up on
   R&D..34
   Who Owns the Design?............................35
The Legal and Political Background to
Manufacturing 36
   When the Village Tells the Factory to Move 36
   When the Government Tells the Factories to Clean Up
   Their Act 38
   More Laws and Less Flexibility 39
   Protection of Intellectual Property.................39
Where is Manufacturing in China Heading? ...40
Lessons Learned 41

Chapter 2
Selling to the Chinese Market: Building a
Chinese Sales Army 43

The Continuing Influence of Mao 44
Understanding the Chinese Market............45
   A Weighty Issue 46
   No Discounts 46
   Price Comparison 47
   Generating Sales Leads Through Gifts..............48
Building the Chinese Sales Army 48
   Recruitment 49
   Using (Altruistic) Communist Ideology.............50
The Right Way to Pay 51
   Poor Performance 52
   Goal Setting, Slogans, and Recognizing Achievement 53
   Adding to the Motivation 53
   Elements of Pay Structure 54
   Tracking Sales....................................55
Training..56
   Simple Training Doesn't Work 56
   Selling Boot Camp 57
   Continuous Learning Culture......................57

Corporate Culture in China 58
Promote Chinese Managers Fast .59
Balancing the Need for Power with Responsibility . . . 59
Being Involved as a Boss 60
Caring and Showing It 61
Lesson Learned 61

Chapter 3
**Start-Ups in China: Get In, Get Money,
Get Out, Nobody Gets Hurt 63**
Going to China 64
renren.com 66
Fund Raising 67
Public Listing 68
Exit 68
Mobile Interactive Games 69
The Start of the New Business 69
Incubation and Trade Sale 70
DragonPorts 71
Kooky Panda 73
Investment in China 73
Getting into Business in China .74
Seed/angel Funding 75
VC Funding 77
Valuations 78
Exit Challenges 79
Lessons Learned 80

Chapter 4
**Negotiating in China: the Great Conjuring
Trick 83**
Negotiating in China 84
Flattery 86
The Personal Questions 87
You're so Rich and Clever... I'm So Poor and Stupid . . 88
You Need Me More Than I Need You 88
This is the Start of Something Beautiful 90
The Endurance Triathlon 93
Trial by Arduous Consumption Survival Strategies . . . 97

Chinese Negotiation: Price. 98
Chinese Negotiating Tools. 99
    Ulcer-Inducing Avoidance. 99
    You Don't Understand China 100
    Splitsies. 101
    Wounded Pride: Street Slang 103
    Getting Past the Gatekeeper. 104
    Not My Problem 105
    Hotel Lobby Negotiations. 106
    Deceit and Making It Up As You Go Along 107
    Imperialist Guilt 110
    Zero Sum Negotiations 110
    The Tantrum. 111
Strategies for the Outsider 112
    Dumb Foreigner. 112
    Show Me Some Face 114
    Write the First Draft. 114
    The Killer Line 114
Lessons Learned 116

Chapter 5
Everybody's Number One Challenge: Human Resources 117
Business Fundamentals .119
The Necessity to Focus on People 121
    Initial Recruitment Strategy. 122
    The Scale of the Challenge. 122
    Retention 123
The Big Change: Laying the Foundations for
Growth 125
    Introducing Family-Style Management. 126
    Building the Business 127
    Introducing Clarity. 128
    Belonging. 129
    Standardization 130
Recruiting and Training 131
    Initial Interviews 132
    Training. 133
    Pay for Talent 134
    Identifying People to Progress 135
    Making the Leap from Staff to Management. 136

Logistical Challenges with a Growing Business 137
   Going National..................................138
   Learning about People: Gaining Some Perspective...139
   Mistakes......................................140
Lessons Learned 141

Chapter 6

Fostering Creativity in China............143

Massive Multiplayer Online Games...........145
   My Introduction to MMOG 145
   The Business Necessity for MMOG 146
   Product or Service 147
   New Phenomenon.............................147
   Why Stay in China 148
Radiance: Forming (June 2005 to June 2006) .149
   Radiance Corporate Structure....................149
   Logistics of Setting Up an Office..................150
   Behaving Like "the Boss".........................151
   Stock Options and Other Ways of Paying People.... 152
   Patience.......................................154
   Chasing Dream Projects.........................155
   Operating in Stealth Mode 156
Radiance: Storming (July 2006 to June 2007) .157
   Bilingual Staff and Cultural References 158
   Employee Turnover.............................160
   Pride in Work 161
   The First Income-Generating Project...............162
   Radiance Enters Expansion Mode..................164
   The German Project 165
Radiance: Norming (July 2007 to June 2008) .168
   Fierce Conversations with Venture Capitalists 168
   Monte's Paradox................................170
   It's All Good 171
Radiance: Performing 172
   The Necessity to Finish..........................173
   The Process of Finishing Game Production 173
   Learning to Criticize.............................175
   Single Issue Focus 175
Lessons Learned 177

Chapter 7
Chinese Style Risk Management: the Need to Diversify **181**

Getting Started in China .183
Moving into Property Investment 186
    Property Development 187
    Commercial Property 187
Growing Out of Real Estate: InnShanghai 188
    Learning a New Business 189
Moving into Hotels 190
    Learning How to Run a Hotel 191
    The Business Case for Hotels 192
    Running the Hotel 192
    Implications for Our Business .193
Business Changes in China 193
    The End of SPACE: The Need to Change 194
    Personal Drivers 195
    Shrinking to Core? 197
    Capitalizing on Confidence 197
    With the Benefit of Hindsight .199
The Notion of Risk in China 200
    The Fear Factor 202
Mistakes 203
    Holding On For Too Long 203
    Not Getting Investment 203
    Partnering 203
    Relying on the Wrong People .204
    Not Acquiring the Right Talent 204
Lesson Learned 206

Chapter 8
Exploring the Road Less Traveled **209**

Setting up Asianera 211
    Choosing Tangshan 211
    New Experiences 212
    Finding a Business Partner 213
    Setting up the Factory 215
Building the Business 216
    Defining the Market 217
Design 218

Intellectual Property 219
The Road Less Traveled..................... 220
Artists 222
Evolution................................. 223
Lessons Learned 224

Chapter 9
Resilience and Persistence................ 227
Groove Street............................. 228
Reinventing the Loyalty Program............ 230
    Initial Loyalty Program Idea...................... 230
    One Card for All 233
Doing Business with Global Players.......... 234
    Market-Leading Innovation 235
    Arbitration...................................... 237
Creating Coalition Loyalty Plans 240
Changing and Evolving the Business Model .. 242
    Smart Friends 242
    Smart Talk: eBay for Non-Physical Items 244
Raising Money for the Business............... 245
    Investor Walking Away 245
    Chief Operating Officer and Losing VCs 247
    The Next COO................................... 249
People.................................... 251
    Loyalty 251
Media and Entrepreneurial Philosophy....... 254
    Win In China.................................... 254
Lessons Learned 257

Appendix
Made it in China: the Featured Entrepreneurs.

Made it in China: the Featured Entrepreneurs. 259

    Bob Boyce 259
    Scott Barrack 261
    Graham Jeal 263
    J C Lim 264
    Grace Liu. 266
    Montgomery Singman. 267
    Richard Robinson. 269
    Paul Stepanek. 271
    Henry Winter 273

Foreword

For businesses outside the country, China presents three key opportunities:

■ **A new market to sell goods (especially consumer goods).** China represents over 20% of the world's population: the world's population is rising, China's percentage of the world's population is rising, and personal wealth in China is increasing, making China a true growth market in every sense and by any measure.

■ **A low-cost manufacturing base.** Chinese manufacturing has become emblematic of the rise in low-cost offshore manufacturing. From clothes to iPods, over the last few years consumers have come to expect falling prices (and for technology products, falling prices coupled with increased functionality). For many companies there is now apparently only one way to compete in this new marketplace: manufacture in China.

■ **A new place to do business.** The booming economy and the industrialization of China have led to many people leaving the land and moving to the cities. This huge and unprecedented change in the largest society in the world has created an extraordinary new place to do business (particularly for those helping to build China's infrastructure).

However, China is different and proud to be different. There are a whole range of new cultural, political, legal, and economic challenges to be faced, even for businesses with experience of the country. It is a confusing market for those who do not understand it: the vast majority of businesses that go to China fail, and fail for reasons they don't ever get to comprehend and many major global organizations have had their fingers burned due to their incomplete grasp of the country and its culture.

Made it in China shares the insights of a group of non-Chinese entrepreneurs who give their first-hand account of their experiences in the country. These are people who have gone to China, invested their own money, got their hands dirty, and have built successful businesses. These people are the real deal and (at the time of writing) are all actively working in (and on) their businesses in China.

Each chapter focuses on the practical experiences of one individual as they grew their company in this new and developing market with each entrepreneur focusing on a different aspect of doing business and talking about their area of expertise. The stories are both practical and entertaining, combining first-hand anecdotes about the challenges they faced and how these were met, with their own observations and thoughts for dealing with each situation.

Introduction

Welcome to China: Understanding China

For 19 out of the last 21 centuries China was the richest and most advanced society on earth. Under imperial domination, civil war, and then the Great Leap Forward, China moved backwards relative to the rest of the world.

The situation within the country started to change in the late 1970s and although the Communist Party remained in power, market reforms were introduced. Since the early 1980s, China has witnessed the longest sustained period of growth in any modern country. Hundreds of millions of people have been lifted out of poverty and a changing world, with China at the steering wheel of the global economy, is taking shape.

For many years China was a well kept secret. At the start of the 21st century the Financial Times and Wall Street Journal mentioned China sparingly, maybe once every couple of weeks. Today, China is mentioned in some way or another every day. After the dot com boom and bust, China has emerged as the next gold rush. History will judge whether this is another economic fad, but the length of this growth period is unprecedented and the shift in the center of gravity of global economic power appears unstoppable.

Coming to China

Most people who now arrive in China find a country that has mapped the shortest and most direct path from Maoism to prosperity, and a country that is surprisingly far down that path.

When people first arrive, they find a warm, friendly, and open country, with a highly-educated population and yet at the same time, in many ways the country may appear quite simple and quaint to the outsider. China is a world of contradiction and confusion. It is one of the world's largest countries, but it is run like a mom-and-pop shop. It's impatient to get rich, and get rich in a hurry. It's eager to learn and anxious to ensure that the foreigners stick around.

For the Chinese people, foreigners are like a canary in a coal mine. While the canary is still singing, the Chinese will be spared a repeat of the more colorful chapters in their history. The Chinese people want and need the modern world, even if the modern world is unsure about them. The Chinese are keen to put the miseries of previous generations behind them and they are in a hurry to do this.

Perhaps the most confusing place is the most international place: Shanghai, the heart of modern business-focused China.

To the outsider arriving in the sparkling Pudong International Airport, Shanghai is a gleaming modern city of freeways, subways, suits, and cappuccinos. However, go into a supermarket and the world changes. There's no chance to buy bread or cheese, but if you want chicken's feet or duck's tongues you'll have no problem. And this is the contradiction that is China. It combines cities with all the excesses and internationalism of Western cities, uncomfortably grafted over thousands of years of doing things differently.

As Richard Robinson notes in his analysis of business start-ups in Chapter 3, for the entrepreneur there is probably no better place in the world to be at the moment. There are opportunities to be found everywhere in this resurgent super-economy and the attractions of China are many and varied. Not only are the opportunities plentiful, but the barriers to entry are low and the cost of doing business is (generally) equally low, meaning that entrepreneurs can take the time to develop their business.

Trying to Understand China

China is vast and has a huge population. It is always difficult to give precise population figures (especially in China where the records may not be accurate in many rural areas), but to give a rough idea of the scale of the population and some comparisons:

- The population of the United States is around 300 million.

- The population of the European Union is around 500 million.

- The population of China is at least 1.3 billion, and by some estimates, it may be as high as 1.6 billion (in other words, twice the combined population of the US and the EU).

Most people who come to China and who have had experience of doing business outside the country find that they have to invest twice the amount of money, twice as much time, and twice as much effort to get half the results they wanted. However, China is a place of such scale and opportunity— even after doubling all of the investments and halving the returns—that it still often makes sense to do business in the country.

To begin to try to start to understand China, you need to get a grip on the country's history and its culture. China is a new country operating in the constraints of an ancient civilization that is fully aware of its place in history. Understanding Chinese history and traditions helps explain the Chinese approach to business. Montgomery Singman explains this background and its implications in Chapter 6 where he talks about the challenges of fostering creativity in his firm.

In order to do business in China it is critical to understand the motivations of the Chinese people and to realize that nothing can be assumed. Only then can you look at training the workforce to work in a modern economy. Bob Boyce discusses this in more detail in Chapter 5 where he explains the development of his family management style, and how it applies to the national restaurant chain he has built.

Dynastic China: the Communist Dynasty

Many people are confused about how the Chinese can wave a red flag and sit behind a bust of Mao and Marx in what is one of the world's most rampantly capitalist states.

This confusion neglects to look at Chinese history where for thousands of years the country has been run by dynastic families. In the middle ages there was the Ming Dynasty and the Qin Dynasty founded much of what we recognize as China today.

Today we have the Communist Dynasty. Mao was the first Emperor and Hu Jintao is the latest Emperor.

The thought processes, decision making, and ways of getting things done in society are surprisingly similar to any time in Chinese history. In today's modern world the emperor and his mandarins have to ensure that the common man is better fed, housed, and educated than in the middle ages, but essentially the same forces shape policy. In Chapter 2 JC Lim gives us a lesson in Maoist teachings that are relevant for business in modern China. He tells us how he has taken the lessons and widely understood themes in Chinese history and applied them to build a Chinese sales army.

Taking the essence of Chinese tradition in another direction, in Chapter 8 Grace Liu tells the story of how she took her passion for Chinese craft and tradition, and turned it into a modern international business.

You Will Never Be Chinese

China is more than a country or nation state, it is a nation continent. For the foreigner learning to deal with this nation continent is one of the biggest challenges. But the foreigner needs to understand that he or she will never be Chinese. You can live and work in the country for 25 years, marry a Chinese person, get a passport, learn the language, have Chinese children, wear the clothes, and wave the Chinese flag, but you will always be a foreigner.

In addition, there are the ethnic Chinese who had the "misfortune" to be born overseas—for instance the ABCs: the American-Born Chinese—who the Chinese firmly believe will one day all flock to the motherland. The Chinese regard these people as ethnically part of the same group, much in the same way that people might be Irish or Jewish—it's a matter of "being" not simply place of birth or religion.

This notion follows through in the territorial integrity that the Chinese leadership has given to China—the Middle Kingdom—throughout history. The Middle Kingdom is as much an ethnic concept as a territorial one.

China Works

There is, of course, much to criticize about China, much in the same way you could identify criticisms of the US or Europe. But there is one unassailable fact—much to the disbelief of everyone who studies the country—China seems to work. If all the foreign-owned businesses were to leave, it would definitely hurt the economy and shave a few percent off of the growth rates, but the growth rate would still be impressive.

It is naïve to compare a developing country such as China to the developed world: we will leave that comparison to future generations. Instead, we point to one of the greatest governmental achievements of the last century, where the Communist party has followed policies that have taken hundreds of millions of people out of poverty. Most people are educated, most people are fed, most people are clothed, and most people have opportunities that simply do not exist in other comparable countries.

The Legal Framework

The Chinese legal system is very different to the legal frameworks in the rest of the world. Equally, the Chinese attitude to the law and in particular, the comparatively new concept of contract law, is very different.

Unlike other countries, there is no Roman law or common law history to the Chinese legal system. Instead, all of the business laws in China have been passed since the country opened itself up to market forces. This means that the most experienced lawyers and judges only have about 20 years' experience and there is no significant history of case law from which the lawyers can draw.

Perhaps the hardest concept for non-Chinese nationals to grasp is that in essence, everything to do with business in China is illegal—*everything*—unless you have a license. In the West, everything is legal unless it is prohibited by the law. In China the government tells you what you can do through the licensing process and so the entrepreneur operates within those constraints.

In practice most business activities are acceptable as licenses can be vague. The Chinese language used is often imprecise allowing flexibility to interpret a license in a certain way which means that any company can be constrained at any time. This issue is illustrated in Chapter 7 where Scott Barrack talks about how he ensured his business is not adversely affected by seemingly arbitrary licensing decisions.

The Role of the Notary Public

Some of the best legal advice comes from notary public officials and not lawyers. Notaries have been working in the legal system for longer than the lawyers. They take a far greater role in China than in the West, and don't just witness things, they provide legal advice that can be better than lawyers can offer, and they write contracts.

Chinese Contracts Are Written In Poetry

If you get a contract translated you may be horrified about how imprecise it is. Concepts that are familiar in the West "you will do this, by then, and if not, this will happen" rarely exist in Chinese contracts. Instead, the terms in a Chinese contract may say "party A causes a troubled feeling to people near party B, money will help".

Think of contracts as being written in poetry and you will start to get an idea. In Chinese contracts, much is left open to interpretation. This is one reason why it is often better to go to arbitration rather than litigation. In Chapter 9, Henry Winter details how he sought and achieved a legal resolution in China through the arbitration system.

There are some important points to understand about contracts. The Chinese believe that the person who writes a contract has a greater obligation to keep to the terms than the other signatory. This is why there are far more "standardized government contracts" and contracts written by notary public officials than you would expect in the West.

Apparent Disregard for Contract Law

Many people have seen a foreigner screaming at their Chinese business partners "read the contract... can you not see what it says in the contract". These people have missed the point.

In the West contracts are seen as a destination: something cast in stone. The Chinese see a contract as a starting point in a relationship—the starting point of a journey. Often the Chinese don't even keep a copy of the contract as they know that everything is subject to revision and discussion as and when things change.

In Chapter 4 Graham Jeal takes us on a journey through the board rooms of the Yangtze delta on a crash course in negotiation with hard nosed Shanghai property developers. As Graham explains, while trying to negotiate a contract is tough, getting the agreement documented can be harder still, especially when a Chinese business partner can't see a necessity for the documentation.

Intellectual Property

The Chinese attitude to intellectual property is very different to the attitude taken in the West. Get over it and get on with your life.

There is little history of copyright or patent enforcement within China. However, in Chapter 1, Paul Stepanek outlines an intellectual property story with a happy ending for one of his clients.

A much better attitude is to acknowledge (but not endorse) the poor practice and work around it: make your business immune to copyright infringement (or other unwanted business practices). In Chapter 5 Montgomery Singman explains how he changed his business in light of the environment, turning the product into a service that generates a monthly income. In this case the reaction to a problem has led to a more robust business.

If You're Going to China… Then Go

If you're going to do business in China, then you need to go to China. You must be on the ground conducting business on a day-to-day basis. Businesses that are managed remotely generally fail in China. You cannot make decisions or carry on negotiations on a one day business trip to China made every six months: you need relationships, understanding, and expertise.

Many of the entrepreneurs featured in this book have found that in their years of working in China no serious non-Chinese competition has emerged largely because nobody sent anyone to come and live in China, get under the skin of the country, and understand how the system worked.

For Western companies, the use of Western advisers that are based in China (in particular in the area of operations) is often helpful, as is employing locals as directors/advisers. But decisions have to be taken daily and based on a variety of factors that you can only understand when you see, live, and breathe China. Successful businesses cannot be run from afar.

However, those who do go should be aware of Skyscraper Hypnosis—a disease that particularly afflicts Western businessmen who come to China gaze around at what has been achieved in such a short time, look starry-eyed at the fancy cars that choke the roads of most major Chinese cities, swallow all of the partnership propaganda, and throw their money (or their company's money) at deals that they would never do in the West.

12   Made it in China

Chapter 1

Manufacturing in China

But for a conversation with a neighboring librarian, Paul Stepanek may not have ended up in China. She told him that the "next big thing" would be China—from that point he set his sights on the country.

Having had some work experience in Taiwan, a friend introduced him to a Mid-West company that was looking to move its manufacturing operations to China. Paul grabbed the opportunity with both hands and helped move their manufacturing facility to China where he remained and ran the factory.

The company grew and Paul got the opportunity to open and run other factories in China. After 7 years it was time for a change and Paul set up USActive, a consultancy specializing in helping foreign financial institutions and manufacturing companies with their initiatives in China.

Paul has considerable experience from his time running the factories and his work with USActive, and is highly sensitive to the issues that frequently arise in China, especially in manufacturing. He has made it in China by making things in China and by helping others to make it in China.

After visiting and working with literally thousands of factories I have found that most of the time we could have reduced the intensive audit process for possible partners for our clients to two simple observations. One—if you can smell the toilet from the front door, or two—if you do not see the expansion plans in the general manager's office, then they are not a viable operation.

These two simple observations often reveal as much as more analytical research can; more quickly and more graphically. If the factory tour reveals that you cannot smell the bathroom from the front door, then the factory probably has good basic management skills. If the general manager does not have construction plans for factory expansion in his office then that is a warning too. In a growing market anyone who is not riding the wave must be doing many things wrong.

Of course, this is a generalization—and the dynamics of the market have significantly changed in 2008. Even so, our auditors have had some fun as they winked at each other when they could smell bathrooms before they were seated in a meeting room.

Getting to China

When you want to go surfing, go where the big waves are...

I was 12 years old when I read an article about Japan being a boom economy. They progressed from making plastic flowers to athletic shoes to electronics and automobiles. Real estate prices and wages were going through the roof. I thought to myself that by the time I reached working age I would have already missed out. I wanted to front-run a boom and I wanted to find someplace which would boom after I had already been there long enough to position my surf board. After speaking with a number of people whom I respected as being worldly—it was clear that China would be that place.

I made my plan. I was going to study engineering—work for a few years—get an MBA or MIM—then work for a few years—and then get sent to China by some company which shared the vision that China was going to be the future. The plan was longer than my patience, so I flipped it on its head. I decided that I would go to China first—learn the language—and then I would have the tools to get jump-started.

I hunkered down, started Mandarin language courses in the US and won a fellowship to study in Taiwan. Back in the late 1980s Taiwan was still booming. It was the perfect place for me to learn the language and have a first-hand look at what the future of China would look like when her economic reforms started getting traction. Taiwan was meant to be a stepping stone in getting positioned in China and so after some years in manufacturing there I quit my job and did a tour of the Mainland.

I visited over 30 different cities to get a feel for what was going on and where. This was the early 1990s and it was clear that the timing was right for the first tier cities. I zeroed in on Shanghai as my target and then went back to the US to get "sent" to China. Now that I had the language and some manufacturing experience I was sure that it would be relatively easy to find a company which I could help to enter China. This proved to be a longer search than I expected to find a fit.

This company had its manufacturing base in southern China, and although this was not my exact target, I justified it to myself since Shenzhen was a lot closer to Shanghai than Milwaukee. So off I went. A handful of factory start-ups later I had made my way to Shanghai.

During these early years I spent long hours making sure that production lines were running and customers were happy. In my free time I was out exploring the countryside, often on a mountain bike. This passion for exploring turned into a hobby which then turned into my first business in China, **BOHDI®** ADVENTURES (bohdi.com.cn), which gets people out to have fun—hiking, biking, and team building.

In 2000, I had completed the set-up of another factory in the Shanghai area. I had always enjoyed the thrill of helping companies be successful in China. I have been successful in doing that on a very tight budget and time line. The excitement of orchestrating all of the moving pieces to create an organization which produces something has brought me a great deal of gratification.

It is a very tangible process: bulldozers clearing the land, contractors constructing the building, hiring and training staff, installing production lines, sourcing materials, product moving out the door. It is very clear if you are making progress and if you have been successful.

There are no half measures here. You are either shipping qualified product—profitably and on time—or not. I had been successful in making it happen for my employer time and again, and wanted to be able to share those skills with all the other companies which would benefit from that knowledge as they too executed their China initiatives—thus USActive (us-active.com) was born.

USActive started out with a very simple vision of helping companies be successful with their China business. It started with the philosophy of creating open, honest, and fair relationships with our employees, suppliers, and customers. Over the years we have expanded our service offerings and geography. We work with financial institutions and manufacturing companies which benefit from our experience and ability to implement and execute in this environment. We have stuck to our vision and our values which have made their way into our processes, so our people are constantly reminded of the excellence for which we are striving.

Communism and the Cultural Revolution

During the period of the Cultural Revolution (from 1966 to 1976) the country was suppressing its poets, sending its scientists out to break rocks, and taking anyone with an education and making them into farmers. People who were highly educated, and may have had many decades of experience, were pushed out to the countryside. During this time there was no real development in industry or business.

In spite of how unfair this seems, it is amazing how resilient the people are who endured such treatment. I have not heard a single bitter story from the people who lived through that part of China's history. They simply say it was the way it was back then.

The Cultural Revolution stopped education for everybody. Coming to do business in China, one will often go into a company and find there are very few people in the office who are over 35 years old. When you do the sums, anyone over 35 or 40 should have been going to school during the Cultural Revolution. The result of the Cultural Revolution is that a lot of people have been left without the advantage of an education. Mao shut the doors to the country and it wasn't open again for business until after the Cultural Revolution.

Since China has opened up for business it has seen the kind of growth in decades that other countries have seen during a century of industrial revolution. With this explosive growth, wages and responsibilities have gone up at an incomprehensible rate.

However, there has been inching progress for people working at a state-owned company that essentially has been frozen in time for 40 years. More than that, these people haven't been trained to cope with this change and having lived for most of their lives under this ideology, they don't have the skills to chase the opportunities that are part of the current day China.

Guanxi-ocracy...

In capitalist societies, people are (to a greater or lesser extent) rewarded for the benefits or merits that they bring to an organization.

During the 40 year rule of Mao, the size of the pie was fixed. The only way to get a bigger slice of the pie was through guanxi—through your relationships. This wasn't meritocracy—this was guanxi-ocracy. As the pie was not getting any larger, people developed and honed their skills for finding who had control of resources and building relationships with whoever could provide what they wanted or needed.

So if Mr Wang was in charge of allocating apartments, and I was in charge of rationing cigarettes, and my wife was in charge of sewing needles—we would make sure Mr Wang's daughter had enough sewing needles and he had enough cigarettes—then maybe he would find us a bigger or more desirable apartment.

People fine-tuned their skills to survive in a guanxi-ocracy. They didn't have a chance to develop technical, managerial, or value-adding skills, or skills to take an organization forward.

In 1979 things started to open up. Deng Xiaoping went to southern China and said it doesn't matter if a cat is black or white, as long as it catches mice. There are different interpretations of what he said, but many people in China interpreted it as meaning "we're Communists... nudge, nudge, wink, wink. We'll keep the spelling..." In other words, it was an end to communism in all but name. Deng's approach was both practical and pragmatic.

After a decade of change the results were impressive: the experiment was considered a success and the opportunities opened further. The Chinese jump-started their economy with light industry and allowed investment with a lot of change coming in through southern China (where the first experimental economic zone was) via Hong Kong.

...to Meritocracy...

With the changes, for the first time in living memory there were people who were finding out that if they worked harder they got paid more. Or if they were a smart engineer that their boss was going to offer ever increasing opportunities, or that they would be able to go and find a better paid job at a place that valued their set of skills.

Suddenly there was a change from the old relationship-based economy to an economy where the value someone provided was rewarded and the size of the pie was no longer restricted. It ceased to be a zero sum game: if you worked hard, it didn't take away work from someone else—instead, everyone got rich—and in the words of Deng Xiaoping, "to get rich is glorious"!

The parents of these children were stuck with all they knew: the mindset that it's all about relationships. Naturally they were fearful—they all had iron rice bowls (in other words, jobs for life)—and didn't want to leave their state-run company because the state controlled their job, their housing, their medical attention, and their children's education. For them, the state was a one-stop provider and there was no perceived safe option for incremental change. Only the extremely brave were willing to try for a position in the new economy.

...to an Upside-Down Society

Despite the parents' practical concerns, the kids were keen to take advantage of the new opportunities. For the younger generation who were not so directly affected by the Cultural Revolution, their worst case scenario—if everything failed—was to go back and live with mom and dad who had an iron rice bowl.

When the kids are out there taking risks, working hard, and earning as much as they can, junior soon started to earn more than dad.

The norm (which is the current situation) soon became that as people graduated they would go and work for private companies rather than state-owned enterprises. These companies are paying a multiple of what state-owned enterprises pay (but obviously offer a different overall package, so for instance, housing is not included). Added to which, how can companies stay competitive if they have people who don't want to or can't change? There are fewer options for people who have never used a computer in their life.

So you reach a situation today where junior can be making 5- to 20-times what mom and dad are making. Usually someone works his way up, and even if he earns more than his parents, it takes a long time to accumulate the assets and wealth of his parents. However, in China today if mom and dad have been able to save anything over the last 40 years, it can be completely dwarfed by junior's earning power.

The net effect is to put the power of society in the hands of those who are making the money, and so in China today, in many instances, the younger generation is in charge.

A practical example of this power can arise if a son offers to buy his parents an apartment. While this may be a kind offer, the apartment will be in Shanghai (or another major city where junior lives) so that the parents can help with childcare. Mom and dad won't necessarily want to go, but they have little option. While their children control the purse strings, parents grin and bear it.

But while junior has the power, he doesn't necessarily have the maturity. Teenagers (and people in their early 20s) will not necessarily make the best decisions: they lack life experience and maturity. They are adolescents and they will do what adolescents do. As the country becomes an even more significant world player, we will all benefit from the additional years and experience.

How to Manufacture in China

There are two main business models for manufacturing companies that want to manufacture in China:

- set up your own factory, and

- contract the manufacturing to an established factory.

There are benefits and drawbacks to both.

Setting Up Your Own Factory

Take a company which has proprietary manufacturing processes, which would like to participate in the global market by selling into China. This type of company would be likely to benefit from having a manufacturing base in China due to the geographical proximity to the market. This proximity would also allow the company to be in closer contact with its customers and to respond more quickly to their needs.

These companies are typically business to business suppliers. An example of this is a company which supplies assemblies to the automotive industry. Any company which considers itself to be a global player must have operations in China. This example company is no exception: it has capital-intensive proprietary manufacturing processes which are critical to their products. Without owning the manufacturing facilities in China its clients would not buy from this company. Period.

These factories are often world-class and, other than the cost of land and labor, are not any cheaper to build and operate than in the developed world.

Contract Manufacturing

On the other hand, contract manufacturing is valuable for fast moving consumables where companies have strong design, sales, and marketing.

This type of company would not benefit by investing in costly equipment or processes that could limit the flexibility of the company. From generation to generation of product, they can find the most suitable supplier (which has the most appropriate processes and capabilities) and take advantage of someone else's existing overhead. This allows the company to leverage the "local knowledge" that a contract manufacturer has, whether that be an ability to maintain a low-cost supply chain or effectively manage labor costs.

An example of this is an earphone manufacturer with highly stylized designs. The guts of the product are similar to, if not the same as, many other brands of earphones. This company lives and dies by making its sales based on having the latest, coolest, hippest designs (and the identity of the contract manufacturer is unlikely to be a consideration for the customer as the customer is buying the brand).

Chinafy the Process

People who want to take advantage of manufacturing in China will benefit by understanding how to China-fy their processes. Equally, they will benefit by understanding the compromises that people will try to make in China and only accept these compromises if they are the right thing to do.

Less automation gives more flexibility. The US, Korea, Japan, and Europe have all put in heavily automated systems for manufacturing. On the whole these systems are not flexible, for instance, if you want to reduce the thickness of the plastic casing for a product, that is not a simple change. This lack of flexibility means that companies in China which tend to be less automated can adapt more rapidly, and following this example, they are able to use less plastic—perhaps only 1 gram less—and so cut their costs. Each incremental change keeps them a little bit ahead in the game.

By having their production lines rely heavily on manual labor, many factories can swiftly adjust for different types of production. It also allows for rapid and easy changes when the component mix changes or when the component design varies.

While this approach may seem counter-intuitive to Westerners—and it is certainly not without its disadvantages—this is the reality of manufacturing in China today. Remember that for all of its many and huge strides forward, there are still 800 million peasants in China: it's going to be a long time before the boat gets floated for that many people.

Of course this approach does mean that costs are going up and will continue to go up. For coastal regions costs—for instance, the cost of real estate and the salaries of manager-level staff with bilingual capabilities—may be nearing Western levels. But there are still a lot of people who would like to see their standard of living rise and so there will still be somewhere in China that will be cheaper. This means many factories will be able to adopt this flexible approach to manufacturing.

As you would expect, by taking a more manual approach you lose something in quality. While it may not fit with the conventional Western approach, if you can take out some of the capital intensiveness and replace it with some manual labor (with a suitable quality process) that is not always a bad way to go.

Managing Growth in Times of Chaos

In China past, companies were able to employ ten people to do one person's job because labor was so inexpensive. The mentality was to throw bodies at a problem rather than take the time to understand the root cause of the problem and systematically remove these issues. In China today, only companies that design an efficient process—and continually improve it—will survive.

The more chaotic and inefficient companies will not fail for a single reason, but for a whole combination of reasons. For instance they will not be competitive because they will not get their processes right, they will not continually improve, they will not get their efficiencies, they will have too high a percentage failure rate, and so on. No one issue will be fatal, but when you add all the pieces together you get a company which will not be able to compete.

In my experience over the last 20 years in China, successful companies are usually the ones who are taking the time to:

■ manage and continually improve their processes

■ manage and grow their people

■ understand their costs and market prices, and

■ grasp how they can add value for their customers.

These are the companies that will survive and thrive. The opposite are the companies who will throw another body at a problem rather than go back and fix the root cause.

Let me illustrate some of the madness that is out there. I was in discussions with a company that is quoting on doing some plastic injection molding. As part of the molding they will build a tool and make parts. One of the engineers said that if the part came out of the tool warped they could put it in a cooling tank and hold it down with cooling fixtures so that it doesn't warp.

He couldn't see that he had just added two or three processes and made the end process less consistent than it could be. We don't want those added processes that will also have a potentially detrimental effect on quality. Unfortunately the engineer was not focused on quality and efficient processes. His sloppy and lazy approach was to throw bodies at the problem rather than designing an efficient method to produce a high quality part the first time. He didn't have the mindset that it would be preferable to build a better tool rather than add more processes to compensate for poor design.

There are many companies and people with this mentality and they won't make it. This issue isn't unique to China, but it is more prevalent with the ready availability of cheap labor.

During recent factory visits near Shanghai, one factory owner reported that one-quarter of the factories in that area had gone bankrupt in the past months. These were mainly metal bashing companies (involved in stamping, forming, and welding). So while there are lots of cheap manufacturers in China, lots of businesses are able to cope and it's the inefficient ones that aren't surviving.

As overcapacity peaked and demand slowed at the end of 2008, we saw many of these less efficient factories simply close their doors for business—probably never to open again.

When the Price Is Too Good

Pricing is a symptom of incredible growth and lack of depth, experience, and maturity within companies. The whole process is incredibly frustrating, but at the same time, while I don't condone the practice, I understand how and why this happens.

How the Quotation Process Works

Let me try to explain what usually happens. Take a typical company that would like to know how much it will cost to have their product made in China. They send an RFQ (request for a quote) to a number of factories. A manager will receive the RFQ (which is likely to be one of many received that day) and will flip it to a 20-year-old kid in the office and say "give me a quote by 5pm".

The kid will be confused, overloaded, and distracted. He will have a stack of quotes on his desk left over from last week and he doesn't know how he will ever get to the bottom of the pile. He will be sending SMS (text) messages to his girlfriend between the eight concurrent chats he has going on his computer screen. He will do an incomplete job and pass the quote to the manager who will glance at it, sign it, and the half-baked quote will go out.

Only if the factory gets the business will they figure out what the customers wants and what it will cost to make it. This is incredibly frustrating if you're on the other end. Unfortunately, this is more often the case than not.

With our clients we will do the homework but we still find that when the first order is placed the factory will say "oh no, we can't do that". Our process involves a manager level employee going through the bill of materials, specifications, and quality requirements—item by item. Even so, we still run into gaps of understanding.

Once the purchase order is placed, it could be months from the initial sourcing and quotes, and cutting a potential supplier loose at that point could leave the project behind schedule. To rectify this situation, we will work through the gaps of communication.

In spite of having a signed quotation, the supplier may throw up their hands and say it cannot be produced for the price they quoted. Sorry.

This brings to mind a recent project USActive handled to manufacture some exercise equipment. We requested pricing from a few factories on behalf of a client. The factory we chose was 40% cheaper than the closest competitor. When tooling was completed the factory nearly doubled the price!

They claimed a variety of reasons from the exchange rate, to material price increases, to a change in labor laws (all increasing their costs).

This was frustrating to us and to our customer. To better understand the options, USActive re-surveyed our supply base and found the other suppliers had also increased their prices albeit not by as high a percentage as the chosen supplier, but significantly nonetheless. Armed with the additional pricing information we were able to let our customer know that even though the original supplier doubled their price they were still within the new market price.

Many Westerners think that Chinese factories are trying to take advantage of a situation. Sometimes they are, but quite often they're not. Often these are honest mistakes because the factory staff are so busy and not necessarily very organized. It is frustrating that companies don't take a higher degree of responsibility or pay greater attention to detail, but that is just part of the game in a hyperactive economy. It is certainly an advantage when you work in China if you can handle a degree of uncertainty and change. If not then you will find China to be a very difficult place to do business.

The Chinese Approach to Contracts

In a Western contract-driven legal environment, the event (a contract) kicks off a process intended to achieve the results. In China, often a contract merely signifies an agreement to work together. Even though there are terms in the contract, these are often considered to be flexible and re-negotiable. It could be mistakes (such as a miscalculation on pricing) or changes in the business environment (material price increases) that will have you back at the negotiating table. When you go back it will be important to bring some "Ps"—patience, persistence and maybe even a bit of practicality. After all—when in Rome…

Renegotiation does not signal an intention to ignore a contract, or to minimize any of its terms, but it is important to understand that the terms and conditions may be revisited many times during its life. Each time the contract is revisited the provisions must be reasonable for both parties.

Working through contract changes in as fair a way as possible will build goodwill and respect on both sides. The relationship is not an event: it is a process. How you engage and handle the challenges that arise will be more important than the signing of the contract.

Management by Walking Around

Another point to remember is that patient persistence is a way of life in China. The squeaky wheel—the nagging—will often get attention. The Western business that tries to operate remotely (without having people on the ground in China) will not be able to keep on top of its contracts and manage the "process" during the life of the relationship.

I have found that when doing business, especially when implementing an agreed contract, it is important to know who you are working with, and there is no better way than being in contact regularly.

It's only by having people on the ground in China, who are regularly in contact with your business partners, that you will be able to verify the common understandings, or to see the earliest warning signs that something may not be on track. I always try to be clear on what I want up front, but the needs of all businesses change. This makes it even more important to have someone understanding and reviewing any changes between partners on a regular basis.

Getting a Proper Quote and the Devil

While it's great being able to understand why quotes are so variable and most people can understand why terms will change during the life of a contract, that understanding isn't much use for a business that wants to get a reliable quote on which it can base its business plans.

So how do you get a proper quote?

The first thing to repeat is that, like many things in China, it's all a process and not an event (you will notice that I've said this before, and I make no apologies for the repetition). It is impossible to take the same approach that you would in Germany or Japan—you will not be able to nail down every detail. We always try to be as accurate as we can but we still have to work with the dynamic environment.

When USActive finds a company that:

- seems reasonable

- has the capabilities, and

- is interested

then we then spend the time. It is important to understand that each quote represents the first step in a process that may end in failure or success. Our team will go out to that facility and will go through the quote item by item, to make sure the company understands what they have quoted. As part of this process, among other things, USActive will go through:

- samples

- the original drawings

- the material specifications

- component lists, and

- function tests.

I have found there is great value in reviewing the specifications or getting them to read the specifications to us. During that review we probe further and ask practical questions—how will you make the wall thickness—can you machine to that tolerance—what equipment will you use—do you have capacity—how much?

USActive is relentless and persistent, and looks at the challenge from as many angles as we can to ensure we narrow down the possibility of any misunderstanding. These questions also help highlight areas where the factory may not understand what is required and at the end of the process we at least know that the producer has been forced to think about what is required.

Also, as we will be receiving a number of quotes, we will be able to notice obvious discrepancies and follow up on these. So if one factory is quoting higher than the others, that may be an indication that they are intending many more manual processes.

The face-to-face interaction opens the door for further dialog where there may be other misunderstandings or where they will need additional information. The only way to get close to a reasonable quote is to get into the detail, make sure that the quoting party understands what they are being asked to do, and then check and recheck. There simply is no short cut. As the saying goes, the devil is in the detail.

Getting What You Order

In two decades of manufacturing in China I have never seen a set of drawings and specifications which matches the samples of the product currently being made. This is not a China problem: this is a manufacturing reality.

This is how it usually happens. Joe designer does the drawings. Bob makes the tooling according to the drawings. Steve starts to manufacture the product and it does not fit together. Steve goes back to Bob and says: part A and part B would fit together if you would make part B a little bit smaller.

Bob obliges, Steve can now make the product, and the boss is happy as they have something to sell.

But nobody told Joe and the drawings do not reflect what is actually being made. So when it comes to the point that the boss would like to outsource to China the company sends out drawings to get quotes. They find some good pricing, they make a contract and place an order, and the product does not fit together.

Nobody is happy. The boss is mad and says "can't you guys make a good product?" The factory fires back "we made it to YOUR drawings".

It seems obvious, but it is imperative to have clear, complete, and correct drawings and specifications. Too often this is not the case and it is the fault of the customer. In these instances, the China factor—with new business relationships, distance, and language barriers—only makes things worse.

Who is to Blame When It Goes Wrong?

To a great extent, I have found that you get what you order in China, but that is the some the world over. However, there are China-specific issues.

The biggest issue is communication: the interface between two parties. Often we just need to get two guys to sit down together in a room and one to explain the issue to the other and for the other to respond. It may seem blisteringly simple, but the root of virtually all problems in China is communication.

As with manufacturing anywhere in the world, hours and hours are spent in meeting rooms trying to figure out what the client intended or what the specifications mean. One thing it would be difficult to do in China would be to over-communicate during the process of getting what you want. However, there are aggravating factors such as the language, the distance from the customer, and time zones that mean that working with the Chinese can be more of a challenge.

If you're a manufacturer and you're working with a tool-maker who might be five miles down the road (as opposed to a Chinese toolmaker who could be a full ocean or continent away from you) then you can go to lunch with him on a weekly basis. If this toolmaker is in China, lunch presents more logistical challenges and so the "how's it going"-type conversations don't happen. The informal back and forth isn't there and so issues tend not to surface. If the issues don't surface, they can't be fixed.

Another important factor to remember is that the Chinese do not (at the moment) have an ingrained business culture which looks to quality and improvement. The default for the Chinese company is "how can we make it cheaper?" The tendency is not to ask how it can be better.

They don't think about adding a bell, a whistle, or some new feature. They think how can we make it thinner, how can we make it faster, how can we slip in some filler so it's less expensive. It is atypical for them to consider added benefits.

Will it change? Absolutely. The reason I can be so confident is by looking at Taiwan, where that country started, and how much they have achieved in everything from processes, products, culture and life.

Think about Honda or Hyundai: these brands have all moved up the chain over the years. It's only a matter of time before the Chinese start innovating—maybe they'll come up with a new drink flavor. Maybe it will be something more conventional like a car design: there are Chinese automobile brands but currently the designs aren't too sexy and the way everything fits together isn't that great. But it will change—and how exciting it is to be here to witness!

Moving From Manufacturing to Innovation

The single most significant factor which is needed for the Chinese manufacturing industry to take the next (huge) step forward is innovation. But this is not a simple evolution: China is a country that has not placed value on design and creativity. There is a joke (which is unfortunately true in so many instances) that R&D stands for receive and duplicate.

In China, companies will copy anything and everything. They will take *any* shortcut to make a quick buck.

The comparison with India shows how far China needs to go on design. To give a simple example, India is able to design (from the ground up) a car to meet a market at a specific price point, and to meet that design aspiration. In China such a notion would be ignored in favor of swifter routes to riches. But again there is the comparison with India where you have family-run companies that are generations old—this means you have the experience and maturity, and there is perhaps a calming effect giving an environment where things happen a little more methodically.

China will evolve and will incorporate design: it's a basic need of survival. It is not just the efficient companies that will survive but those who are able to create. To take the next step forward China needs to be able to make components designed with an understanding of what the customer wants. Until that happens (and it is happening) China will remain a copy shop—a place where "I can do it cheaper" is a louder voice than "I can do it better".

R&D is coming, but it is part of the evolutionary "development" process—there is little research currently underlying this development. As Western companies get their product directly from the manufacturer in China there is an increasing trend for Chinese companies to recognize that they could be the company to bring a new product to market.

Artisan Class

To design, China will redevelop an artisan class.

This is where the damage of the Cultural Revolution shows. They stole the wind out of the sails of a whole generation of people who were teaching the youngsters about their experiences. These were people of many talents: painters, poets, writers, engineers, business men, and lawyers. This means that people aren't able to reach out to an older generation—there is no one with grey hair that can share their stories and give sagely advice.

China is slowly getting back that culture. It's going to take a while to rebuild—to get a generation of people who have learned a skill, who have developed a skill, and who have managed people with a skill. As part of this they need people who have developed a well-defined interest in something beyond the notion of financial reward. Currently the focus is on money.

Eventually the artisans will resurface. These people will be less focused on money and will be passionately focused on doing what they do better simply for the beauty of their end product.

Moving Up the Value Chain: Westerners Giving Up on R&D

A big mistake made by some Western companies who outsource their manufacturing is to give up on R&D. I can best illustrate this with a few examples.

Take Schwinn bicycles: this used to be the only real bike brand in the US and was a major seller. Every kid growing up in the US had a Schwinn bike (me included). The company designed and made bikes and sold them through mom-and-pop bike stores.

Schwinn found that they could make bicycles cheaper in Taiwan and so they outsourced their manufacturing. Then

Schwinn got lazy and asked their manufacturer to design the next year's models, and so the manufacturers took on design.

While this was happening, the world started to change. Mom-and-pop bike stores started to get competition from "pile 'em high, sell 'em cheap" big box retailers. The world of bike selling changed: you don't need to pay a premium for a product that just needed its tires pumped up.

Schwinn was locked into a declining network, it had lost design control, and the manufacturer then decided that not only could it manufacture bikes, it could also design and sell under its own brand (Giant) and sold the bikes through big box retailers. It was a near perfect storm for Schwinn.

That evolution is a typical scenario for many products and industries. Several things happen at once: the sales channel goes from intimate to mass market, and the company that used to have manufacturing and R&D at its core has given up those core skills to become a sales organization.

There are many similar stories. I know a hand tool manufacturer that was founded on a deep understanding of what its customers wanted. Then they got someone else to make their tools for them. This was fine. Then they decided that their manufacturer also had some interesting products and so instead of designing their own products, they filled out their own product line with some of their manufacturer's other products. And in so doing, they lost a core competency—design.

Who Owns the Design?

As well as giving up on design, other companies don't make the right investment and see things through. Often this is naivety about intellectual property ownership.

Usually what happens is a company comes up with a concept, but they don't want to pay an engineer to take that concept to drawing, and then from drawing to prototype, then back to the drawing board a few times to get it right. Instead, they start with a concept and work with a Chinese company to get it made. During the process, the Chinese company will develop a set of drawings and make incremental improvements on the design and tooling to make the product functional.

So who owns the design?

The foreign companies think they have prior art. Chinese companies think "you haven't paid me a dime, not for revision 1, not for revision 301. Do you have a set of drawings?" It's at this point that the foreign customer gets angry and frustrated, then looks meek and humble, and slightly scared. It happens again, and again, and again.

Retaining the intellectual property is important, as is making the investment in research and development.

The Legal and Political Background to Manufacturing

Underlying the day-to-day working relationships with any Chinese manufacturer, there is the Chinese legal and political background. China is a country which is seeing huge changes, many of which are intended to rectify years of disastrous and destructive government policies.

As a country, China has a deep hunger for the future and is racing to that goal as quickly as it can. In this race some people are getting trampled underfoot. However, to balance this, there is a maturing view about the necessity for the rule of law and the consistency of the law's application.

When the Village Tells the Factory to Move

With the rate of development of the country, and more to the point, if things are going to change quickly enough to pull the huge population out of poverty, then some changes need to me made "for the greater good" which may have short-term negative implications for individuals. These changes are a regular occurrence.

A client of USActive had eight years left on a long-term lease on a factory building. The village government came in one day and said "time to move". A year later after dragging our feet and negotiating we were able to get a settlement which left our client with RMB1 million in the bank after paying for the move related costs.

Situations like this do not always come down to legal or moral arguments. However, there will usually be some compensation when the other party is not fulfilling its obligations. The best approach is to take the compensation and get on with life. There's no point in moaning because no one will listen or care. In the case of our client's factory, the moral of the story was to not be in too much of a rush. Use the time to investigate alternatives, use the "Ps" to your advantage and wear them down with some of your own persistence. In the end you will likely be able to work out something that works for both parties.

Again, the comparison with India is enlightening. Because India has democracy, the authorities can't say to people that this week's rules of the game have changed and it's time for you to move. Instead if you want a road to go from A to B in India it will take a decade of consultation. In China by the time you've turned your head, the road is built from A to B and they're building from B to C and anyone who was in the way will have received some sort of compensation—and the road will get completed.

At this stage in its development, China is being quite fair and quite pragmatic: the alternative is not to develop. They need this pragmatism to make things happen and the court system doesn't slow things down. The other factor to remember is that the country is run by engineers: people who have been trained to make things happen and who are therefore the best people to be in government. Compare that to the West where government is run by lawyers and movie stars.

The outcome of this approach is that China has been able to develop (in particular its infrastructure) very quickly. For an example of this, look at Shanghai where they are building a 26 square kilometer transportation center at the domestic airport. It will have a magnetic levitation train station, numerous train lines, hundreds of bus lines, an airport, subway, and light rail. It will be the largest human transportation hub ever built in the world. It started in 2007 and will be finished before the Expo in 2010. When China puts its mind to it—they will make it happen—and on time.

When the Government Tells the Factories to Clean Up Their Act

It's not just the village governments that have an impact on businesses.

USActive undertook a study of plating companies. As part of this study we identified over 550 different plating companies in a region. Subsequently the government decided to crack down on polluting companies—the impact for plating companies (who are big polluters) was to require them locate their facilities in a government run industrial park. The park would then handle all of the waste water treatment so that the pollution problem could be addressed and there would be no option for any company to cut corners.

From 550 companies, the government decided to allow 20 licenses. The transition from 550 to 20 was introduced over a five year period. The effect was to force consolidation, but it also made sure companies obeyed the law. Naturally, the long-term effect is China will be a greener place (albeit a more costly place to do plating).

More Laws and Less Flexibility

The law in China is black and white (and there are plenty of laws). However, the way the law has been applied varies. There are many laws that have always been there but the enforcement has been patchy depending on the region, or the people involved, or a particular political hot button. Currently there are first generation lawyers and first generation judges: the guys on both sides of the big desk have the same limited experience. This will evolve and mature, but it's not there yet (and thank goodness it is not as litigious as America!).

In addition, as the country opens there is a need for different or more relevant laws, and so the law is evolving and will be enforced with greater uniformity. There will be more transparency, more relevancy, and more consistency. As anywhere, the laws, their relevancy, and their enforcement will be a step or two behind development, and as China develops its legal system it will narrow the currently large gap.

Protection of Intellectual Property

China—quite rightly—has a reputation for ripping-off intellectual property: the notion of receive and duplicate is justified and that label will probably stick for the coming decades. However, the practice is changing, albeit slowly, and there is a growing appreciation for intellectual property rights with an increasing respect for the laws that enforce these rights.

As Chinese companies develop their own intellectual property and want it protected they will force the system to become fairer. This will happen with the growth of the artisan class.

However, all is not lost at the moment and there are other avenues for companies who have had their intellectual property rights violated. It does take a concerted and comprehensive approach to enforce the protection as we recently found out when we helped one of our clients.

We were dealing with a US company with world-wide patents (including for China) that was producing a component that could be easily copied, and the component was being copied by Hong Kong and Chinese companies. We identified the main knock-off producers and selected the weakest. We then hired a local Chinese lawyer and set-up a bonus scheme for the lawyer so that he would be well rewarded if we collected.

USActive assisted with information collection and helped with a media campaign. We also prevailed upon the US Consulate to apply pressure and make it a political as well as a legal issue. The outcome of hitting the problem from a lot of different angles was good: we won our case and collected a substantial sum.

As far as I know, at the moment this approach is still fairly rare. However, it is getting easier to fight this battle. It's not every day that the foreign company is successful and the stories are not always happy. But the rule of law is getting stronger.

The even happier ending came the next week when we licensed the five other knock-off producers to give our client an ongoing royalty stream.

Where is Manufacturing in China Heading?

Every week I get asked whether there is a future for manufacturing in China. The short answer to that is a resounding YES!

The longer-winded version of that is as follows. As the market environment changes, China is becoming a relatively more expensive place to make things (relative certainly to where it was 10 or 20 years ago). Costs have been increasing in US dollar terms and otherwise. The exchange rates are making it more costly to export.

Changes in government policy discourage high energy consuming and high polluting industries (through a reduction in the sales tax export rebate). Those industries are being forced to reform or relocate. Recent government policies which place more of the employee benefit burden on the company also increase the cost of operating in China.

At the end of 2008 we are seeing most of these factors being reversed—at least for the near-term. The exchange rate has stabilized. Sales tax rebates are being increased and material prices are coming down. China will continue to allow the pendulum to swing in this direction for the near-term.

Longer-term, all of these trends can be expected to continue. China would like to, and will increasingly move to, higher value-added types of manufacturing and services forcing the lower level types of manufacturing to other lower-cost countries.

That being said, China is a massive country with an enormous population. There are millions of people eager for a job, and it is those people who will continue to keep the China manufacturing engine churning out product for a very, very long time.

Lessons Learned

There are many lessons to be learned to have a happy manufacturing experience in China.

- First off, it is difficult to over-communicate. Communication has nothing to do with what you say: it's all about what the other person understands. Take the time to make sure that the other person has understood. Communicating properly includes following up on a regular basis to ensure that the understanding is reinforced through the process.

■ As well as communicating, make sure that the information you are supplying is correct. For instance, check that any drawings you send to China reflect the product you want built, and not the product as it was originally designed and before you made the changes that actually make it work.

■ The costs in China can be so much lower than they are in Western markets and the desire to outsource to China is often driven by costs. This encourages cost cutting in all areas of the business. You cut every cost you can at your peril.

■ Lack of control of your research and development—in particular, if you don't make the necessary investment so that you are controlling the development of a product after it passes to your Chinese counterparts for manufacturing—equates to giving away your intellectual capital. Unless your strategy is to continuously out-innovate the competition, this may not be a smart move.

■ Patience and persistence do pay off. Whether setting (and maintaining!) the vision and values of your company or dealing with suppliers—patience and persistence have always proven to be effective.

Chapter 2

Selling to the Chinese Market: Building a Chinese Sales Army

JC Lim's entrepreneurial career was nearly cut short before it began.

He was born in Malaysia and went to Sydney, Australia to study accountancy and finance. During his time in Australia, in a show of youthful high spirits and bravado, JC placed a bet on a horse race and lost nearly all of his fees. It took many hard hours working in the fish market to earn back the money to pay for his education.

JC began his working life as an auditor in Malaysia, moving to be an internal auditor for a cookware company. In this role he was shocked to see the salary figures for the sales force. Having been embarrassed at having to borrow money to buy a girlfriend's birthday present, he decided to make a career change and try sales.

After a shaky start, JC found that he had an aptitude for sales and rapidly became his company's highest achieving salesman. He so impressed the company that they sent him to Hong Kong where he was appointed as the sales manager and was charged with turning around the failing business.

He achieved this turnaround, but after a restructuring decided to strike out on his own and persuaded the company to allow him to sell their cookware in China. They agreed and since then JC has seen over a decade of 30-50% year-on-year growth and his sales force grow to 500 people.

I'm a student of history and believe that history always repeats itself, and so I believed (and continue to believe) that China will repeat its past successes.

When I was living in Hong Kong, I felt the vibes. More Chinese people were coming into Hong Kong, and more and more people in Hong Kong were going into China and setting up factories. Subconsciously this reinforced the message that something big was going on.

When I first went to China, my expectations as to what was happening were exceeded many times over. At the same time the backwardness was a shock to me. For instance, there were hardly any decent restaurants (especially when compared with Hong Kong where you get so much variety and choice). A lot of the restaurants were state-owned and would close at 5pm or 6pm—the restaurant would literally close for dinner.

The streets were very dark—so dark that the first incentive that I gave to my sales people was a high quality flashlight so they could see their way. I would never have thought about giving that sort of sales incentive in another country, but I soon realized that achieving success in China would require me to re-educate myself on the business of sales.

The Continuing Influence of Mao

Mao got to know China by roaming through the countryside and meeting ordinary people. He developed a deep understanding through his inquisitiveness and his analysis.

The important issue to understand in China is working with the masses. When the Chinese fought the Japanese, Mao had an inferior army. He didn't have weapons, but instead he had people. The only resources that China has are people, so when I set up my business, my thinking was that if I want to sell here I should do it with a lot of people.

It's also important to understand the kind of people that Mao recruited. He didn't look for the type of people who would be suitable to work in a Western-oriented multinational corporation. Instead he took everyone and used them to the best of their abilities. He recruited the peasants—and lots of them—and repelled the invaders from the borders. This has been my approach to building a sales force and has allowed me to find some very good people who don't fit the conventional mould.

The way Mao pulled in the people was with ideas: he gave them a sense of mission. When I am building a sales team I try to give them a sense of mission—you and they have to believe in the future. Mao led people with the ideology that there was a better future even though the people were so hungry that they were eating tree bark and the roots.

I have adopted and adapted many of Mao's ideas and have found they serve business well in China.

Understanding the Chinese Market

When I started the business in China, I took the stance of the typical businessman who had done well in other countries. I looked at the market from a foreigner's point of view and with a foreigner's ignorance. I was a typical "laowai"—the semi-derogatory word the Chinese people have for foreigners or outsiders who come to China.

I started selling the combinations of cookware that were sold in the rest of the world at the prices that would be charged in the rest of the world. We were successful to a certain extent, but it took a lot of work: you might have to do ten demonstrations to sell one set. That is a lot of work for one sale which was leading to sales people becoming demotivated.

A Weighty Issue

Because I was basing my strategy on everything I had learned outside of China, I was happy to send the sales team out with 20 kg (45 pounds) of sales kit to demonstrate. This isn't an unreasonable amount of kit outside of China as everyone has a car. However, in China people tend to get around by bicycle which means that 20 kg is far too heavy. With Shanghai being so geographically huge, we were finding people had to cycle for far too long with a really heavy bag.

Again, outside of China, potential customers tend to live in houses which mean that you only have to lug 20 kg from your car through the front door. In Shanghai people tend to live in apartments which meant that after cycling across town, the sales force would then have to carry the product up several flights of stairs. Added to which, apartments tend to have less space than houses.

Clearly something had to change—the configuration of the sets and the Chinese market did not match (and they were also wrong for the sales force). So we made the sample sets smaller and lighter (about 10 kg) which meant that it became easier for people to carry the demonstration sets on their bicycle and these were more appropriate for customers' lifestyles.

No Discounts

Some people asked for discounts and I always told them that we had a no discount policy. This meant that I was fighting the market while trying to protect the company and the brand. Again, I was looking at the position from a foreigner's perspective which was all I knew.

The Chinese haggle: from the little old lady on the street selling cherries to the school child buying a lollipop—everyone haggles and negotiates. Negotiating is not optional—it is part of the sale—and the Chinese expected something that I was failing to accommodate.

In the end I found that there was no point in trying to fight the market and so I built an offer into the product. I still refused to give a price discount, but what I would do was give a free upgrade to a bigger pan. I also gave away a cookbook and would usually throw in something else for free.

To put things in perspective, the value of the upgrade and free goods would be equivalent to about 10% of the sales price which would be better than any discount I could offer.

Price Comparison

It was only through understanding the market that I got a better grasp on how the Chinese think.

There was one occasion when I was trying to sell to a customer and he said that the set was very expensive. So I asked him what he meant when he said the equipment was expensive. I then asked him what he was comparing the cost to: you cannot compare the cost of our cookware to regular household cookware since ours is of a much higher quality.

His retort took me back: he was comparing the cost of the cookware to the cost of his house—the cookware was *half the cost of his house*. This was an argument I had never come across before and was a situation where I had little ammunition: the salesman in me was literally lost for words.

Of course, as I got to understand the environment, it became clear that the comparison was not completely balanced. In the state-planned economy many people were paid a low wage and were given subsidized housing. Some people who had lived and worked in a particular place for a certain length of time were given the right to buy their house at a very cheap price.   So this individual wasn't comparing the cookware with the market price of his house, but rather the heavily subsidized price.   However, the customer's perspective, and my need to understand the different circumstances of the Chinese customer, opened my eyes.

The flip side to this was when I went to another formerly state-owned house.   The house was quite run down but it became clear that the couple had a big house or a luxury apartment somewhere else.   The run down house was very convenient for their work and was near to some good schools. These people clearly had a second source of income from the gray/black economy and kept huge sums of cash under their bed.

Generating Sales Leads Through Gifts

The sales people are responsible for generating their own leads, but we help them to expand their leads.

Everyone likes to receive a gift, however in China giving and receiving gifts is a central part of the culture—there are many festivals where specific gifts are given from cakes to red envelopes of cash.   It is also part of the culture that people often try to turn down gift when they actually want it.

When we sell a set of cookware, we will allocate a percentage to cover the cost of a gift.   The sales person can then redeem this gift to give to their customer.   The customer is then given a gift that they can share with their friends.   Our approach links the Chinese culture of gift giving with the referral problem.

Building the Chinese Sales Army

When we hire people for our sales force, we don't require a certain prescribed skill set—in many ways we might be seen to be a lot less choosy than multinational companies.   Where a lot of companies may bring in expatriates, we don't have the resources to do that and we don't believe it is right for our business.

Instead we recruit people who understand and can empathize with the people they are selling to. Typically these people do not speak English (not that that skill is necessary). As I said earlier, as someone with a keen interest in the country's history I have learned many lessons from Mao which I have then adapted to my business, and in China, working with the masses is the key to sales success.

Recruitment

There are huge numbers of unemployed people in China, including university graduates. This was more so back when I started in 1996 since a lot of state-owned businesses were shutting down.

With so many factories shut down there was a project called Project 4050: this was a project for people between 40 and 50 years of age who would have worked in the same factory for many years. Often when these people finished their education, under the planned economy they were immediately sent to work in a factory where they remained until they found themselves unemployed following the closure of their factory.

These people have a poor self-image. No one has trained them to do anything except work in a factory. For many, although they have been retrenched (made redundant) they are still paid (since if you don't pay these people there will be another revolution).

When I started recruiting, I was amazed at the huge number and variety of applications. Some people turned up in pajamas (in semi-tropical Shanghai it is common to wear pajamas on the street), some arrived with the label still on their suit (thinking it looked trendy and might be a designer label), and it would be common to receive literally thousands of applications for each position. Because of the one child policy some mothers are so protective of their children that they will go to the interview to prevent their child being exposed to any harshness or rejection.

My approach to recruitment is to sell the company and to sell the product (which is a German product and so is perceived as having a high value). We then select only those who show enthusiasm and eagerness to sell.

As a business, we tried to be prudent and started small. With this basic image a lot of people were skeptical so we had to work on our image and to paint ourselves as being bigger and more significant than we were.

With Project 4050, there was a television program—a bit like American Idol or The Apprentice, but in reverse: the candidates choose the employer. I participated in this and out of three contestants, two chose us. The program was good for our image: whenever someone comes for an interview, we can always refer to that program to help the recruitment.

We also raised our profile by getting our adverts onto the television screens on the Metro. We ran the adverts for one day and recorded when the ads were shown—we then played the video in our offices so we could look like a more significant company. It was a very low-cost way of building our image. The Chinese emphasize image, and so in addition to helping our recruitment, this helped reinforce people's pride in the company.

Using (Altruistic) Communist Ideology

A lot of the income we pay is commission-based: this helps and hinders recruitment. It helps by having an unlimited upside, but hinders because the basic pay is less than the potential upside (even though we pay a good basic level). So our recruitment and retention hook isn't just the money.

We tell people how the great work that they do is important. They are repeatedly praised for making a big contribution to the health and well-being of the society. Using our product gives people a healthy way of cooking which doesn't use oil, and you don't need to boil vegetables (where the nutrients are usually lost in the water).

I believe that people have to understand that there is a greater purpose to what they are doing. Giving people a purpose can have a greater influence than money and helps foster their enthusiasm for, and commitment to their position. This was a big thing for many people—they actually felt that there was a meaning to their lives. We have been very successful with this approach.

It is crucial to understand the people's past in order to understand how they approach work: one key is to understand the iron rice bowl (or job for life) mentality. Within the state system lots of people got promoted because of their relationships (guanxi) or because they had been there for a certain time: ability really didn't matter.

We were able to turn that around by removing the relationship-based advancement system and showing that reward is linked to personal performance. It's the same argument that communism used, but applied in a wholly different manner. We show people the blueprint: how they will succeed, how they will be promoted, how they will become a manager, how the company will grow, and how they will have a career. We can say that their future is guaranteed with us, provided they are performing.

The Right Way to Pay

Despite the common perception, China is not cheap when you consider the total cost of employing staff.

I have the mantra of never having poor people in the company. We have a minimum salary for our sales force. Where many companies will have a sales force working to a minimum commission, we set a good basic wage (which is conditional on meeting certain minimum standards) and then pay additional commission on top of that.

Our minimum wage is five times the level of the government mandated minimum wage. I could set the minimum much lower, but selling is a tough job and I want it to be rewarding. Added to which, as I said, we don't have poor people in the company—they just create a negative atmosphere. I don't want to pay cheap: I want to give my employees a good life. We have no poor people and hence (for us) there is no revolution.

We also pay on a four-weekly basis. This means there are 13 salary payments in a year which is much like getting a monthly salary and a bonus equivalent to one month's pay.

Poor Performance

The factories give out reprimand notes to poorly performing staff. The reprimand note then goes to the employee and a copy goes to the accounts department and a deduction is made from the employee's salary. We have a similar practice for non-performance, but in a more diplomatic way.

The first time that the minimum sales performance target is missed, we issue a "letter for discussion" on white paper. The second time a sales performance is missed, we issue a letter on yellow colored paper to express our concern. The third letter comes on red paper and is when we end the employment relationship.

Through this system we maintain a very high standard and everyone knows the process.

Goal Setting, Slogans, and Recognizing Achievement

We are very big on goal setting. With the planned economy everything was planned, so goal setting is a well-understood principle.

We like to say that people can make 10,000 RMB a month. This is important when understanding China. The Chinese government is good at managing society with slogans—when a phrase is repeated sufficiently, it becomes an ideology.

A lot of Chinese people could repeat all of the sayings of Mao Zedong as written in his Little Red Book some 50 years ago. Today a similar approach is used to educate the public: when the government wants to get an idea across, they bombard the public with so many slogans that people end up subconsciously digesting the message.

Deng Xiaoping said let one portion of the country become prosperous first: it is such a big country that we can't solve all of the problems at once, but at least we can start with a proportion of the people. So we said, let's create a portion of the people who can earn RMB 10,000. When anybody hits that level we recognize their achievement.

When the first person in the company achieved a cumulative income of RMB 1,000,000 we celebrated big time with everyone at the company. He was the first millionaire in our company. It took some years, but it was still a proud moment.

Adding to the Motivation

To help people we always try to make things fun.

I believe that the Chinese concept of face or personal honor is very important. We instill a healthy competition between our employees by exploiting the concept of face. We promote employees, rank them and invite them to special meetings because of face. When you rank people it becomes a big thing.

We have contests with overseas trips, for instance to Singapore, Switzerland, or Australia, as the prizes. We even did this in the early days when it cost us a lot of money that we didn't have. We did this to instill a sense of elitism in our people, many of whom had never traveled outside of China before. As a result of the rewards, our people perform at a higher level.

We had so many beautiful stories of people getting their first passport and their first trip on a plane. We made a celebration out of getting a passport and found that giving pocket money for trips is a very popular and well-received practice.

I have also increased motivation by creating competition. This can be competition with other companies, competition with other regions, or competition with other countries.

Elements of Pay Structure

Unlike Western practices, there isn't simply basic pay and commission. Instead pay is structured as a number of different elements which reflect historic practices in China.

In the factories they would give oil, salt, and mooncakes during the Moon festival. With us, payments are split into many categories, for instance, the pay may include:

- Allowance for nutrition.

- Filial fund: a fund to recognize the Chinese practice of sending money back home to parents.

- New Year allowance: to recognize that people might need to buy some new clothes for the holiday.

- Festivity Fund.

- Transport Allowance.

- Communications Allowance so that people can get themselves a cell phone.

- Entertainment Allowance.

The allowances all fluctuate with sales: they are a part of the sales bonus that is then split.

We retain people with high incomes and also have quarterly, annual, and long-service bonuses. If an employee serves for a quarter and has met minimum standards, we pay a bonus. Equally we pay an annual bonus. We also put a percentage of any sales' commission into a three year and a five year account. After three years we then give the employee the value of this account as a lump sum.

Splitting the payments helps people to see how their pay covers their expenses and obligations. Moreover, while we are a foreign company, our knowledge of Chinese culture and priorities allows us to assume a Chinese identity with our employees.

For the special fund to the parents, a percentage of the income based on sales is retained in a separate fund. During the Chinese New Year, the employee writes a "letter of love" to their parents and the company sends the money to the parents in their child's name. This practice supports the Chinese culture of the strong family bond, builds wider family support for their employment, and again adds to our Chinese credentials.

Tracking Sales

There is only one piece of information that people need to give us to qualify for commission: the number of demonstrations undertaken.

The sales are tracked through the centralized delivery process (the delivery person is employed directly by the company). There is no computer to manage the sales team:

all it would do would be to generate a lot of pointless reports. All I care about is how many people the sales force sees, and how many units are sold.

Training

There are three elements to creating a high-performing organization:

■   the culture

■   the pay, and

■   the training.

Let me share with you something about our training.

Simple Training Doesn't Work

An early mistake I made was giving a simple training. I then gave people their name card and said "off you go" and when anyone didn't work out, we terminated them. A lot of people came and a lot of people went. This meant that we weren't building any momentum.

We realized that part of the high failure rate was related to the background of the people: in the planned economy they had very limited exposure to the type of product and to this type of selling. With the planned economy, people did not have to sell. The factories produced what was necessary and people bought what they needed.

We had to give people time to grow and to understand how different things were. This was especially the case when we were hiring people under the Project 4050 initiative.

It is really important to develop an understanding of people's experiences and not to assume they have had exposure to the consumer society. To remedy this lack of experience, we developed our Selling Boot Camp.

Selling Boot Camp

Our Selling Boot Camp is a really intensive training process to help people become high performing sales representatives in China.

People don't have creativity because they don't know what there is to be creative about: creativity was never a value that was cherished in China. You can't tell people to think outside the box: they don't have that level of understanding of the concept. You have to first give them the box and then move forward from there.

This lack of creativity is also a huge advantage with sales training. People want (and need) to be told what to do: they need to be told every detail. This allows you to ensure a high level of consistency between different individuals and to maintain quality.

So for instance, there is no point in telling someone to call a prospect and make an appointment. You have to tell them word-for-word what they should be saying. You have to tell them how they should say their greeting, how long they should pause, and how they should ask for the time of the meeting.

With this understanding we developed the Little Red Book of Selling in China.

We wanted to make ourselves as Chinese-like as possible. In the Chinese school system, children can recite many classic Chinese poems: the memory of these poems stays with many people until the reach adulthood. These people obviously have an excellent memory. We took these techniques and applied them directly to our sales force. We made the sales people practice so much that it started to come out naturally.

Continuous Learning Culture

As a sales person there are many things you need to learn. As a junior manager people then need to learn a whole new set of skills around how to lead, and as a higher manager there are a different set of skills again.

In China, the leaders have to study the ideology of Deng Xiaoping, the thoughts of Jiang Zemin, or the teaching of Hu Jintao. Every year the Chinese leaders take one month to study.

In the whole country, everyone has to sit an exam: the scholar exam. The very best would be destined to become a member of the cabinet or similar, perhaps become a mayor. Parents put huge pressure on their children to perform in these exams.

This studying and constant learning is something very strong in Chinese culture. We picked up on this idea and have kept the notion of constant learning and linked it with personal development in the country.

Corporate Culture in China

I do not want my colleagues to view me as an outsider who has come here to take advantage of the Chinese, earn a lot of money for myself, and then leave.

I have been very cautious not to look like a rich person. When the business first took off, I could have bought a car, but I didn't for eight years. This issue is a big deal: you don't have to pretend to be poor, but if the staff see that the boss is rich and is earning a lot of money while the sales force is struggling, this sends a bad message. The right message to send in China is that we are here working together—we are striving together for a better future.

This is very much a "hearts and minds" approach and our corporate culture goes beyond money and how we pay people.

Promote Chinese Managers Fast

We promote Chinese managers fast because as foreigners we will never completely know how the Chinese people think. Chinese people know the Chinese mindset much better and can therefore manage Chinese people far more efficiently than a foreigner can.

The Chinese people are nationalistic. There is a lot of national pride in the country. The people respect foreigners on the surface, but behind your back, they are not so complementary. To your face it may appear they think you are superior—underneath they *know* they are superior.

Status and face are also very important. Accordingly, I needed to promote the Chinese locals very quickly so that they can maintain their face and achieve status. Coupled with this, title is very important: it is very important to be invited to a meeting as it implies that you have a status and you are different. Promoting people and giving them a feeling of importance gets them more committed.

Also on the social level this approach helps a lot. When you have promoted your own managers you have your own support group.

Balancing the Need for Power with Responsibility

There is a history of Chinese people getting promoted, then putting up their feet and waiting for the sales to come in while they start ordering people around. We do not want that.

We have to balance the power-hungriness with the modesty that was taught by the leaders of the previous era. There is a Chinese expression, *Wei Ren Ming Fu Wu*: serving the people wholeheartedly. This is very important. People should feel that they serve in a leadership position and not abuse the post.

People need to be accountable. Government meetings always have a work report and this is another Chinese cultural idea that I have adopted. This is a self-criticism system to ensure that managers are accountable for their actions and are not abusing their power. Every quarter they have to stand in front of their peers to give this work report. Typically they will have to humbly suggest:

- three things they have done wrong

- three things they have done well, and

- how they will change their behavior going forward.

This brings in a balance: at one end the Chinese are power-hungry and status driven, but at the other end there is a self-balancing system to warn of any potential abuses.

Being Involved as a Boss

In the early stages of the business I was very hands-on, very micromanaging. There is a benefit to micromanaging: you are demonstrating that the person you are dealing with is important. This carries a lot of significance and helped me to build relationships.

Instead of just dealing with the layer of management immediately below me, or immediately below that, I still make sure I also deal with people at the sharp end. As a manager, I do not hear about the problems of and between people because the line managers will want to guard the face of anyone with a problem. So sometimes (once in a while—not all the time) it is good to micromanage as I can get to hear about issues I wouldn't otherwise hear about.

This approach also allows me to have a relationship with certain key individuals or other players to find out what's going on. It allows me to find information and through this direct communication with people, I can send the message that I am not just a high-level person locked in my room.

Caring and Showing It

Relationships are important, but for me the relationship with the sales force goes deeper. Much deeper.

To give an example: I had someone who broke his arm and I didn't call him. To my mind this was not unusual: the head of a Western company wouldn't usually call when a salesman breaks his arm. This was a big mistake. As a result I've now got a system in place so that this sort of information can reach me.

This is something I take very seriously. For instance, when somebody passes away in a family, we don't simply send flowers—there is a system set in place so I can call the person and let them know that I am sending my condolences personally.

It's not necessary to have a direct contact everyday; however, the lines of communication must be open.

Lesson Learned

I cannot stress how beneficial it is to learn from history. History teaches us so many things.

- The history of the Chinese people shows their resilience and adaptability. Find how to use the talents of the people you have rather than look for people who fit a preconceived notion. Enthusiastic people will always make the best employees.

- Care for your people and get involved—it shows when we're faking it. However, remember you are the boss. By acting as the boss, as well as being able to maintain your authority, you will also be able to show greater respect to your staff.

- When you come to deal with the Chinese market, your product should be appropriate for the Chinese people. You should develop the product for the market (and not the other way round). In addition, you should understand the logistics of getting your product to your customers.

- Take the time to train people properly and then make the training an ongoing process.

- Beyond the training, be sure to link the work to a bigger cause so that people can see a purpose for their work beyond the necessity of a pay packet.

- Try and work in the Chinese way and not the Western way. It makes life so much easier.

Chapter 3

Start-Ups in China: Get In, Get Money, Get Out, Nobody Gets Hurt

Richard Robinson's focus as an entrepreneur is in creating new businesses—mainly in the mobile and internet sectors—focusing on the sweet spot where media/entertainment and disruptive technologies intersect. He's done this a few times and to that extent you could describe him as a serial entrepreneur.

Rich is not the sort of person that you're likely to find plodding along in a large organization as another cog in the machine. He's tried that, but is happiest when he's building companies. This means working with limited resources and out of a small office: at the time he was first interviewed for this book he had a ninety square meter office with twenty employees. This new start-up beehive atmosphere is one in which Rich thrives.

Currently Rich is the CEO of a business he co-founded—Kooky Panda Ltd—which creates socially connected casual mobile games using Flash Lite. In addition to this he is an angel investor and board member/advisor to a number of companies.

He has other interests including acting as a director of another company he co-founded called DragonPorts that specializes in porting games between different cell phone handsets. He is also the co-founder of ChopSchticks which brings Western stand-up comedy and sore abdominal muscles to ex-pats in the Middle Kingdom and across Asia Pacific.

After graduating from USC in Los Angeles in 1989, I spent three years working my way around the world as a waiter in the Virgin Islands, a bartending ski bum in the Swiss Alps, an English teacher in post-revolution Prague, a house painter in Norway, a Grape Picker in France, and a BMW assembly line worker in Germany. From there I took the train from Prague to Moscow, through Siberia and Mongolia, to Beijing and upon arrival I had a China epiphany. The dragon swooped down, as it were, dug her claws into me and hasn't let go since.

I then went to get my MBA at the Rotterdam School of Management in the Netherlands and had a second epiphany while working in the school library. The predecessor of the Netscape browser, Mosaic, had just come out and I surfed the web for the first time and was hooked. I decided to combine my new-found love of China with my addiction to the internet.

Going to China

I then completed a summer internship at the Hong Kong Trade Development Council's Amsterdam office and they sent me to Hong Kong for a couple of weeks. While there I tracked down a friend from my days as a ski bum in the Swiss Alps. Woody Allen once said, "eighty percent of success is showing up" so since I knew I would have somewhere to crash in Hong Kong, I decided to do some more travelling before just showing up there to find work. After graduation with no job, little money, and up to my neck in student loans, I set out to do a solo mountain biking trip through Africa: four bicycles over four thousand kilometers with four courses of antibiotics over four months (but that's another chapter in another book).

I moved to Hong Kong in late 1996 with the intention of working in the internet industry, but unfortunately someone forget to tell the internet industry to show up there before I did. At that time there were very few web users in Hong Kong and perhaps 50,000 internet users in mainland China. After five months of hitting the pavement and freelancing, I was overstaying my welcome crashing with my buddy when I saw a web development agency from New York interviewed on television talking about their intention to open a Hong Kong office. It was my chance to crack the industry and I hounded these guys until they had no choice but to hire me.

Even though we were a satellite office of a larger company, it was a very entrepreneurial environment, so I got to cut my teeth and learn the practicalities of setting up an office, from building desks out of IKEA legs and sheets of plywood, to wiring up the computers, down to learning to hire the right people.

Over time we grew this team to about 45 people and I got to work all over the region doing development and internet advertising for blue-chip clients such as IBM, Intel, Citibank, and HSBC. The company went public on NASDAQ and although I was low on the totem pole, I had my first taste of a liquidity event and it was a start which gave me some capital.

Around this time I co-founded an internet networking group, called IandI (internet and information). Initially, there were around 20 or 30 internet geeks who got together in Hong Kong once a month for some beers and a chat, but by 1998 the group could expect about 90 people to attend a presentation and network. This number continued to grow and we built up to a database of about 20,000 people attending events in 15 cities around the Pacific Rim.

Funnily enough, The South China Morning Post in Hong Kong wrote an article suggesting that these events were a good a place to meet future dot com millionaire husbands. There were definitely some hookups from these events, but I don't think anyone actually cashed out... At the peak in Hong Kong, 300 to 400 people were turning up to weekly events to see speakers which included the founders of Yahoo!, Sohu, Alibaba, and Excite, among others.

renren.com

The dot com boom was reaching a feverish pitch and as a co-founder of these IandI meetings, people suggested that I should set up my own business. At the time there were SysAdmins (system administrators) who knew some HTML and were getting funding. It was suggested I do the same since I was a dot com veteran with the rich experience of a whopping 17 months in the industry.

I wanted to start my own gig, but I knew I just wasn't ready and was worried I would get funded and then drive the company into the ground. Before I started on my own I wanted to learn how to run a real start-up from the inside.

A chance meeting with two former McKinsey consultants at an IandI meeting gave me an opportunity to do just that. The two founders, Michael Robinson and Anthony Cheng were bright, solid guys who had spent months writing a kick-ass business plan. They had a great elevator pitch: GeoCities for the Chinese. Nowadays the elevator pitch would be Facebook or MySpace for China, but at the time GeoCities was hot:

they had become profitable, listed on NASDAQ, and then got acquired by Yahoo! for billions.

The founders had raised some seed funding, had a great logo based on the Chinese characters in the name, and a terrific URL: renren.com (in Chinese, renren means everybody). They were going to provide online community services such as home page hosting, chat, bulletin boards, and so on to the global Chinese community based out of Hong Kong.

I had some experience with internet advertising and had started the first Hong Kong chapter of the Internet Advertising Bureau, so we met to discuss the state of the online advertising industry. By the end of the meeting it had been agreed that I would join as a founding executive and become the VP of Marketing and Sales.

It was a wild ride and I sometimes felt that I had bitten off more than I could chew. There were 100 hour weeks and I often felt like I was drowning, but I loved every minute of it. I was sleeping in the office some nights, showering at the gym, and then putting on one of the dozens of renren.com T-shirts I had piled under my desk. But the upside of being in a start-up was that I got to compress five plus years of work experience into a couple of years.

Fund Raising

One good lesson I learned by observing the fund raising process while at renren.com was that angel investors were important in getting introductions to solid venture capital firms—this knowledge helped to establish the company on the right path.

The company raised $6 million in an A Round, half of which was allocated to the initial advertising budget. We then opened up offices in Silicon Valley, New York, Taipei, Beijing, and Shanghai. Within a year of that we closed a B Round of $31 million with News Corp participating in the round, and Rupert Murdoch getting personally involved in the due diligence process and his son James sitting on our board.

Public Listing

The company then took that second round of funding and did an immediate back door listing on the Hang Seng Index in Hong Kong by purchasing a publicly listed company which was in decline but had clean books and no debt. After taking control, we made that company a subsidiary of our parent effectively making us a public company. While we were now publicly listed, there was no IPO process so no additional funds were raised, but the company was now liquid and we could use that position to make acquisitions by buying other companies with paper.

During that reverse takeover, for one brief, shining (crazy) moment our market capitalization was around US$1.5 billion. I had about 1% of the company by that time but, because we'd done a reverse takeover, we were all locked up for one year and couldn't sell. NASDAQ crashed soon after and so we all "lost" millions of dollars that we never really had in the first place, but it still stung. In any case, we still had a market capitalization of several hundred million dollars, so we were able to snap up some other companies and ended up buying five companies in total.

My team grew to over 75 people and I had an advertising budget of nearly $12 million. I'd never had an advertising budget of more than $50,000 before and the average internet advertising budget I had previously managed was in the region of $10,000 to $25,000. I got through by using the lesson I'd learned of hiring people better than myself. It's a good lesson.

Exit

I moved up to Beijing with the company to drive sales, but we just couldn't make any money. We had terrific traction with solid services, a really well-known brand, a great team, and a loyal and rapidly growing user base, but we just couldn't get advertisers to pay. We weren't alone—at that time the major Chinese portals were all hurting and were in danger of being de-listed from NASDAQ.

We ultimately ended up getting acquired: just as we had done a back door listing, another company did the same and bought us.

Not exactly a graceful exit, but an exit nonetheless which afforded us the opportunity to go and do other things on our own. I had started a business a few years before—ChopSchticks—putting on comedy shows in Hong Kong for ex-pats, and so I decided to professionalize that. I also took some time off to study Chinese more thoroughly and then I bought an around-the-world ticket.

Mobile Interactive Games

I got the inspiration for my next business from my assistant at renren.com. She earned less than 2,000 RMB a month but happily spent 2,400 RMB buying a new cell phone. She would then lovingly adorn her phone with stickers and dangling trinkets, load it up with ringtones, and then spend the whole day sending text (SMS) messages to her friends.

The Start of the New Business

Compared to Hong Kong where the voice market was wildly competitive but mobile data was one notch above smoke signals, the mainland market was really taking off and this was clearly a business where there was a lot of money to be made. I had got a lot of valuable scar tissue from my time at renren.com where I had been working all hours, getting involved in all aspects of fund raising, operations, and managing my teams.

The three biggest opportunities in wireless data were ring tones, graphics, and then mobile games. The ring tone market is tough since the record labels control the licensing. The graphics market is essentially just a picture on a phone, so it is difficult to differentiate. But with games there's an opportunity to create and own your own intellectual property.

Incubation and Trade Sale

Through some friends I met a partner at a business incubator called MINT (Mobile INTernet) which was part of PricewaterhouseCoopers consulting. Working with MINT, I became CEO of MIG (Mobile Interactive Games). This incubator relationship gave me an instant company, access to office space, infrastructure, and staff. All I had to do was build games, run the company, and do deals. I had some capital from my time with renren.com, so I took no salary and worked for equity.

MIG started creating text-based games since SMS was the only viable billable platform on China Mobile and China Unicom at the time, but we always had an eye towards Java mobile games. There was a start-up in Australia offering SMS services similar to what we were doing. They had just closed a round of funding from investors including Sun Microsystems which invented and licensed J2ME (Java 2 Microedition) which is now the leading platform for mobile gaming globally.

After their funding, Sun nudged that company to buy a company in China so they could hit the ground running in what was the biggest mobile market in the world. We were that company and so we got fully acquired in a stock swap, and I was then locked-in for a year. MIG became the number one player in the mobile gaming space in China and was ultimately acquired by NASDAQ-listed Glu Mobile in 2007.

DragonPorts

For a short period after MIG I took the position of VP of International at Linktone. Six months later the company listed on NASDAQ becoming the first pure-play wireless entertainment company to do so globally.

I found myself the last laowai (foreigner, or more literally, old outsider) in the company. Being the only foreigner or one of the few foreigners in a Chinese company, even one as young, dynamic, and nimble as Linktone can be frustrating. Theoretically, as a foreigner, you can act as the bridge between the Chinese and outside markets—in practice you're more like cartilage getting crunched between the realities of the China market and the expectations of international markets.

This is mostly a losing proposition if you can't have control, which encouraged me further to become an entrepreneur again, but I was constrained by the "golden handcuffs" after the IPO.

Fortunately in the internet and wireless space in China it is very cost effective to start a new business. China really is a terrific place to start a new company and I believe China is the entrepreneurial heart of Asia, and Beijing is the Silicon Valley of China. I believe my future is leveraging my new home town as a low-cost, high-skill development base from which to push my wares around the world. This environment led me to co-found a company called DragonPorts on the side while still at Linktone.

When I was at MIG, I found there were three muscles of a mobile gaming company: creating the games, porting the games, and marketing the games. Everybody on my team wanted to flex the first and the last muscle by creating and marketing games, but nobody wanted to make the games compatible for different handsets. This is called "porting" and it involves resizing graphics (to fit different screen sizes), adjusting for bugs inside handset versions, modifying the keys on the handset, and so on.

MIG was porting to fifty or sixty different handsets at the time and while the industry was touting standardization to address this, I knew from experience it would get worse before it got better. I felt that any company addressing this issue properly would provide a pain pill to the industry and have a shot at success. I knew that if I assembled a team and got some investors, I could help to drive business for the company through my relationships in the industry.

I played basketball with an Israeli friend named Ori—a really terrific, scrappy player (I think you can learn a lot about somebody's character when they're being a weekend warrior playing sports) and knew that one of the best traits for an entrepreneur was scrappiness and persistence. Ori agreed to be a co-founder of this company we called DragonPorts—we invested a very small amount of money and found some other angel investment to kick start the business with about $33,000.

The upside of an outsourcing business is that the company can generate revenues immediately, but the downside is that revenue growth can be very linear with a "work an hour, bill an hour" approach. Also cash flow becomes an issue when new handsets have constantly to be purchased to maintain an up-to-date stock.

DragonPorts has attracted some very high value-added angel investors who have contributed immeasurably to the efficiency of the company's work flow. The company's main institutional investor has also stepped up again and again to counter the cash flow issues.

The company has rebranded itself to eMrazor and has expanded its services to include game development. It now has nearly 80 staff, close to 600 handsets, and some impressive clients including Electronic Arts Mobile, Disney Mobile, and THQ Mobile.

Kooky Panda

My latest venture has thrown me back into the mobile gaming space. I was constantly talking to my wife about the Japanese mobile market and what could be learned from there. Flash games on mobile phones had become a wildly successful phenomenon and phones outside of Japan were also starting to get Flash Lite (the pre-installed, pared down version of Flash for mobile phones).

She thought it was such a good idea (and also to shut me up) to get into the mobile Flash space that she started a company herself called Kooky Panda. Just like I always hired people better than myself, I did the same in marriage.

We'd both learned that the more milestones can be checked off, the more a company's risk reduces, and the higher the valuation, so we decided to run this company with a budget of US$40,000 and go as far as we could. The company was able to last for one year on that $40k and made lots of mistakes but learned lots of lessons while creating over sixty Flash Lite games and applications.

I jumped on board after that one year as CEO with my wife as COO (the first time in history a CEO reports to the COO...) and we raised a round of funding with both angel and institutional investors. Each investor brings very solid industry experience and relationships, and has the ability to contribute easily three-times the cash value of what they have invested through strategic directions and introductions.

Investment in China

As well as starting several businesses, I sit on the boards of several startup companies, have also invested in companies as an angel, and have helped companies raise angel and venture capital. Here are some thoughts about the fund raising environment here in China with a focus on the information technology industry.

Getting into Business in China

In many areas, particularly in the internet and wireless technology-related space, it is becoming much cheaper to start something up, especially compared to the dot com boom of the late 1990s. Since the dot com boom times it has become dramatically cheaper to start an internet/technology company since hardware costs have plummeted and open source software has become ubiquitous. This isn't simply a China phenomenon, but with the "China price" helping to keep costs down and the natural entrepreneurialism of staff (if properly cultivated), then it's not just cheaper to start a business in China, but it's also cheaper to fail here too.

When I say "fail", I don't mean "let's start auctioning off the furniture on eBay" or failure in any conventional sense: I mean experiencing a series of significant, but not life threatening, failures and through that process getting incrementally closer to success.

From what I have seen, there are very few successful startups which are doing exactly what they set out to achieve in their original business plan. In practice, over time all companies need to adjust their business plans (sometimes dramatically) so they can bring in new ideas. Many die before they can find the right path.

I believe that operating out of China gives companies perhaps not nine lives, but at least a better chance than in many other markets. A significant advantage in China is that you can do a lot of learning for a very low cost: the iterative process of rewriting a business plan is something that is much more feasible in China compared to many other places in the rest of the world. Plus there's a captive local market that can be tapped into for both learning and revenues.

In China, funding can go a much further than it would in, say, in Silicon Valley. I have a good friend here in Beijing who told me that he'd recently invested in a startup with five other internet industry insiders. The total investment was about US$500,000, but he felt that it was the equivalent of a $3 to $4 million A round in the US.

Seed/angel Funding

While there is a glut of venture capital that has flooded China in the past few years chasing the largest internet and wireless markets in the world, I believe there is a sizable gap in the angel funding space. This is partly due to the fact that it is so cheap to start a company, and partly due to the fact that the market is fairly nascent.

Anecdotally, outside of China "family and friends" financing rounds are in the $10k to $100k range, and angel rounds of up to $1 million are available to qualified companies. Venture capital firms then address the $5 million round and above. Where the gap is mainly found in the West is in the $1 million to $5 million round.

Here in China I believe that the gap is in the $100k to the $1 million round. There's a ton of bootstrapping taking place in the $10k-$100k zone (in other words, entrepreneurs using their own resources or going to friends and family to get things started), but above that range things get challenging for entrepreneurs.

Seed funding is available of course, but just not in the same widespread organized, institutional way as is in the West. There are limited formalized angel networks but the market is growing with the introduction in the past couple of years of angel investor groups such as AAMA and CBAN. There are also some veteran entrepreneurs who cashed out during the internet boom who have invested in some companies, but these individuals are still few and far between.

There are HNWIs (high-net-worth individuals) outside the industry who have seed funded some tech startups and are looking to tap into the potentially rich returns in the space. However, I've had some interactions with companies seeded by such individuals and while VCs conventionally tend not to want to get a controlling stake in the company (to hedge their risk but also incentivize employees), I've found that many times these HNWIs want to control the company in which they invest right from the get go. Clearly this has (usually negative) long-term consequences for the company and the (lack of) motivation of the entrepreneur.

In 2007, I met a Chinese start-up in the online photo space and liked the business model and their founder. I thought I might be able to help them raise money in a later round of funding, and act as an advisor in return for equity. It turned out the CEO of this one-year-old company only had 5% of the company and the angels had 95% with one high-profile angel in the dairy industry owning 85%. I felt it would be impossible to convince an international investor to come in with the CEO holding such little equity so walked away.

While outside of China I've typically seen startups give away 20% and potentially even up to 40% of the company in an angel round, when there is an under-developed funding scene, the people with the money become a lot more powerful. This makes the "angel" moniker pretty ironic.

But in any case, the challenges around funding are less a reflection on the talent in China and much more a reflection about the stage of the market both on the management and the capital side. I see a lot of highly talented and very aggressive, naturally entrepreneurial people in China, but there simply aren't enough experienced start-up executives to go around. Because Chinese companies are especially founder-driven, and due to a lack of well-developed cadre of middle management, the risks for investors increase dramatically which results in a demand for more equity.

Companies looking for seed funding in China will very often bootstrap. In China, you can live on a penny and a big dream. I agree with William Bao Bean, a partner at Softbank China and Indian Holdings based in Shanghai, who believes that: "a US$30,000 per month burn rate in China is equivalent to a US$300,000 burn rate in Silicon Valley."

Due to the low costs in China, many new businesses are avoiding angel funding altogether and are only looking for outside financing when they have proved their business concept works.

VC Funding

While there are challenges with finding angel funding, by comparison, there is almost a glut of venture capital funding in China. According to Zero2IPO.com.hk, in 2007 US$3.25bn was invested by VCs in China (up 82% from 2006) with 42% of that or US$1.38bn invested in IT across 202 deals.

Within the technology sector, there is disproportionate availability/allocation of funds according to geographic location. Kaiser Kuo, Director of Digital Strategy for Ogilvy China, who is a fixture on the digital scene here in the Middle Kingdom, estimates that roughly 60% of funding comes here to Beijing, 30% goes to Shanghai, and the remaining 10% is spread among the whole of the rest of China.

This is partly a reflection of where the industries are based, where the talented people are located, and the fact that Beijing is the seat of government, but that isn't to say that there are not opportunities elsewhere. In many ways there are parallels with other well-known entrepreneurial hubs in the US such as Silicon Valley and Boston's Route 128 which have created a virtuous funding cycle within their borders.

Like other hot spots, there is an influx of foreign money in addition to the home-grown finances. Some of the companies that made early and big bets in China have made a considerable return (which they are now reinvesting). The success has prompted others to try to follow suit.

At the moment, the venture capitalists I see in China tend to be less specialized and more generalist than in the US or elsewhere in the world. In general VCs in China have not been that innovative—they have looked for me-too investments in ideas that have worked in the US and are being localized for the China market.

Technology-related deals are less attractive to VCs because of the high pricing and lagging entrepreneurial skill sets in these areas—this lack of skills is a significant issue. In addition, technology innovation is much less developed and, I would argue, not widespread in China, and so Venture Capitalist are driven towards proven business models and technologies in China.

While the aversion toward technological investment is perhaps counter to the original concept of technology VC investment, this will change. As China inevitably takes advantage of its engineering talent, universities, and industrial base to become a technology innovation powerhouse, the specialized tech VCs will come to the fore.

Valuations

As of the first half of 2008, Chinese start-ups had the highest pre-money valuation in the world: their value is higher than Silicon Valley or London-based companies. A typical valuation will be $9 million at the time of the first professional investor (A round) and $23 million for the B round.

However, I see one significant differentiator between Chinese and non-Chinese companies: usually when a Chinese company goes to raise funding it will be much further along the curve than its Western counterparts. Typically in China there will be higher user numbers, higher revenues, and so on.

One reason for these high valuations is the excess local capital coupled with strong foreign investor competition: the availability of both sources of capital in such quantities pushes prices up—supply and demand applies in China as much as it does anywhere else in the world. In addition, the inflated expectations of domestic consumer spending growth force up both company valuations and company spending in the pursuit of better talent, new products, and distribution.

Of course, higher valuations do not necessarily equate to better quality. In China it seems that companies need to show more, but given China's lower costs, it is easier for companies to "boot strap" and find other ways to get themselves further along the development curve before they need investment. This can mean that the companies are genuinely worth more.

Exit Challenges

The exit routes for investors in China are not necessarily as straightforward as they are outside China. One reason is that for a Chinese national it is not always so easy to sell a Chinese company and expatriate profits to outside the country. Therefore many companies doing business have a local company to employ staff but keep their income-generating company offshore.

Foreign listings have certainly increased dramatically over the past decade with markets such as Hong Kong and London seeing an increase in IPOs. Many companies look for an overseas player to buy them to enter the market, with eBay, Yahoo, Expedia, and Amazon all making acquisitions and investments in the internet space, some with much better results than others. While this option provides a possible exit route in certain circumstances, the same issues arise as with investment in China, such as transparency, management depth, and adherence to international standards.

Domestic merger and acquisition activity has been relatively limited in comparison with the number of funded companies since many of the larger players have had so much organic growth, they've been less inclined to buy growth through rollups (where several small companies are acquired and merged), but that could soon change.

Lessons Learned

- China is a cheap place to fail: you can bootstrap a company and burn for a much longer time while you figure out your company's "destiny". As anywhere, the more milestones that can be reached, the lower the risk and the higher the valuation for future rounds, and China is a great place to tick off those milestones.

- The captive domestic market is large and growing. China is the largest internet market in the world and has the largest mobile subscriber base with 3G services soon to launch (at the time of writing). While it's viable to build a large user base and gain considerable experience, the market is hugely competitive and very well funded.

- Monetization can be a challenge but certainly not impossible. Having a solid China story can help with future fund raising.

- China is a great outsourcing destination. Thomas Friedman got it right when he said that China will not be content with only being the world's factory and leaving India to be the world's office. China wants to be the world's office and it is starting to drink India's milk-shake. Getting a few lieutenants who can speak English to coordinate with partners is key to leveraging China as an outsourcing base.

Chapter 4

Negotiating in China: the Great Conjuring Trick

In this chapter Graham Jeal draws on his experiences when setting up and building Shanghai Vision, a property investment company which attracted over 500 property investors from around the world and grew to have over US $200 million of assets under management.

Graham is a British entrepreneur who founded Shanghai Vision in 2002. Before going to China he worked for the international investment bank JPMorgan in the City of London, New York, and Hong Kong. He also created the Euro China Consulting group in 2007, a consortium of companies with interests in market entry, sourcing, and investment in China.

While in China Graham found himself negotiating with developers, property management companies, staff, and officials on a regular basis, and learned the tricks of the trade at first-hand. He is now a veteran of smoky rooms, the extremes of endless Chinese meals, lawyer tantrums, and some dubious negotiating tactics.

The Chinese understand that business deals are not fossilized in contracts but by contrast are live animals with the process of evolution speeded up. My experience has taught me that the Chinese are probably not good negotiators, but they are masters in the art of haggling. For the business person who is used to conventional (Western) strategies, such as looking for a win/win solution, China is a bewildering place.

Negotiation goes to the very heart of doing business in China: in practice, there is no separation between "negotiating" and "doing business". Trying to identify the dividing line is like trying to identify what is the coffee and what is the cream after you have stirred. You know both are in there—and you can see the respective influences of each part—you just can't tell where one starts and the other ends.

Equally, for many Chinese, there is no separation between private life and business, so your private life will become a weapon or a weakness in the negotiating arsenal of your business partners whether you like it or not. In many ways, this is not surprising: the Chinese believe you need to become friends first and then do business. All things being equal, the world over people will prefer to do business with people that they are friendly with. But in China, it would not be unusual to say "what's the price for the contract" and "would you like to meet my niece" in the same sentence. As a negotiator, the skill is in deciphering at what stage your friendship lies.

Negotiating in China

For me, negotiating in China began when we had an introduction to one of the country's largest developers. By this stage we had already had a couple of false starts trying to relieve developers of the burden of selling their buildings. After several years in China, I am now fully accustomed to the Chinese standard operating procedure of making one feel honored and humbled that my unworthy investors' money might be considered to buy an exalted and prestigious Chinese building. But at this early stage, I was wondering what was so different about my investors' money.

I read up on my negotiation strategies and was primed. I had sat down with our lawyer—who was a Western-educated native of Shanghai—in advance of the discussion. Still I was unprepared. I guess I should have detected this by the rather confused look on my lawyer's face as we went through various strategies and backup positions.

Although this was to be a very different negotiation to others I was to sit through, it was a great place to start as it shattered all of my expectations about negotiation in China. While we had prepared in the way Westerners would usually prepare, it was all pointless.

We went into seven or eight meetings with one guy who was an archetypal cardboard cut-out Chinese middle manager: he seemed to be smart and comfortable in his new but ill-fitting suit and un-ironed shirt, sitting on his leather chair behind his oversized and cluttered desk. He was probably only promoted to his position because he had been with the company for a period of time—it was certainly not because he had ever achieved anything other than not getting into trouble throughout his career.

Only after a number of meetings, when we thought we were nearing a deal, did we find that we were actually nearing the opportunity to sit down with someone who could make decisions. The guy we had been negotiating with was just a courier of information to the decision maker. It was extremely difficult to find that I had spent the last few weeks with someone who was deceiving me about his importance and lying about his ability to make a decision.

Many people have a lot of experience in negotiating. However, negotiations in China—like most aspects of business in China—are different from the rest of the world, I believe. While the purpose of negotiations may be different, within China negotiating tactics can be remarkably similar, and often have the following stages.

Flattery

In 2005 we were negotiating to buy over 120 serviced apartments in a prestige development located next to Shanghai's first yacht club. The complex had excellent leisure facilities, shops, and grade A office buildings: it was (and remains) a beautiful development and an excellent long-term investment.

The negotiations lasted around six months and before that it probably took us two months before we could get to the stage of being able to negotiate. We were negotiating with the project manager of the development, Mr Zhen. In true Chinese style, he was not the owner of the company, but the owner had delegated power to him. The owner sat aloft of the messiness of the organization, showing up occasionally in his custom built Roll Royce with the sole purpose of appearing magisterial.

It worked.

Mr Zhen wasn't just the project manager and the chief negotiator, but he was also the architect, the head of procurement, the head of sales, the head of human resources, the head of crisis management, and the guy who was woken up at 3 am when a typhoon hit Shanghai. In short, he did absolutely everything, including bringing the fruit for us to devour during our negotiations.

However, fundamentally, he was an artist—a creative person. He knew what he wanted and that was to build something beautiful. On this aim, he succeeded.

During the negotiations flattery was used to an absurd degree. We had literally hundreds of meetings with Mr Zhen and the same charade started every meeting, even if we had only seen him a few hours earlier:

...please tell us how your brilliant business is coming along...

...it must be great being so talented and wonderful at what you do...

...it is a real honor to sit across the table from such an amazing person...

This level of flattery became the Chinese equivalent to the English talking about the weather. In my view there are many occasions where the other person cannot mean their compliments or be interested in what they are saying. The comments are simply a way of breaking the ice: it's a dance and everyone is expected to perform, without cringing.

I have always felt that this approach was part of the game, and so I complement back. Often I will say that they must be clever to have built such a company (after all you want to do business with them, right?). Alternatively, I would identify something obscure about the building that I liked, or simply say I thought he was looking good and move on.

Anyone who is not expecting this performance might actually start to think that the other party was truly honored to be dealing with them. Don't believe it. My staff pushed me to complement the other emperor about how well their empire was performing. The other emperor would then always reciprocate.

The Personal Questions

The Chinese have no separation between private life and professional life. Further, it is common for a company executive to live in the office or factory. The work/life balance concept has not made it to China, and in my view is seen as something of a Western absurdity.

After some time spent trading honors we would get down to business, but the charade would always end with an unhealthy interest in my personal life. I found that questions about my marital status, the timing of my having a family, and offering introductions would be as normal as any other question.

In my experience a lot of Chinese business relationships are held together by personal relationships that may have evolved over many years—sometimes it is not worth asking too many questions, and it is worth even less to answer too many questions.

You're so Rich and Clever... I'm So Poor and Stupid

You're so rich and clever... I'm so poor and stupid is a variant on the flattery technique. Surprisingly (or unsurprisingly, if you're cynical), massaging Westerners' egos must work because the technique is so readily deployed.

I heard the "you're so rich and clever" argument sparingly in my dealings: it's hard to make a case of being poor when you have just built a multi-million dollar development, but not beyond the reach of the more creative Chinese negotiators.

I adopted several simple retorts to this approach. Perhaps the most straightforward is to remind the person who is suggesting China is a backwards country that the country can afford to put a person into space. This plays well to the Chinese notion of pride and is very hard to argue against.

You Need Me More Than I Need You

The Chinese are experts at making you believe that they have lots of options and that you need them more than they need you. In my experience, things always started to hot up when I heard words to the effect of "you need me more than I need you".

If you are ever in a situation of thinking you need your partner more than they need you, then you are in trouble and you are likely to find yourself begging to do business.

Begging is the opposite of negotiating: once you are begging, you will never get a good deal. This chapter is not a chapter about begging, it is a chapter about negotiating. In practice, of course, it is important to appear to negotiate when you are actually begging, rather than begging when you're trying to negotiate. Reread that sentence again—in my view, it is both the most important and ill-written sentence of the chapter.

Westerners are used to market economics and the forces of supply and demand, where prices will fluctuate depending on the availability of the product and the number of potential purchasers. Theoretically, prices will rise until there is only one bidder left.

Unfortunately many Chinese show a breathtaking level of carefully cultivated arrogance. I could be offering to bring them many tens (or hundreds) of millions of dollars investment and yet their negotiating strategy would be to suggest that I was the lucky one.

There are several reasons for this attitude. One is the price controls that are mandated by the government. This means that developers become concerned about raising their prices too much as this would draw attention to them. Therefore, the market does not find its own level.

Furthermore, when dealing with government companies, the profit motivation is rarely important. Many people in these companies will not be interested in a profit: they simply want an easy life or not to make a noise that might be heard by the authorities. I always considered it ironic that in such a noisy and boisterous country as China, silence is coveted so widely.

In certain industries it is easier to see how the "you need me more than I need you" attitude arises. For instance, in property there is a finite supply of land—they cannot manufacture any more land in downtown Shanghai. This can lead to an unhealthy level of confidence on the part of the vendor.

Whether you are a client or a vendor, you will be made to feel as if *you* are honored to be doing business. With a property company, it always amazed me how developers would explain how privileged I was at being given the honor of discussing buying their development—akin to some blessing such as inheriting the right to purchase the Forbidden City or the Garden of Eden.

On occasions with Shanghai Vision I was under pressure from David Cunningham (my Western-based business partner) to deliver deals that aligned with our key investor-facing periods. I reflected on how I could negotiate without looking as if we were begging. In summary—and this sounds clichéd but it is a reflection of what we did in practice—the more we wanted a deal the more we made it look as if we had alternatives.

With some of the deals we showed up with literature, figures, and business cards from other deals. In one deal for a development in the north of the city overlooking a park, made with an overpoweringly confident government developer, I deliberately arranged a call with a rival deal to coincide with a meeting I had. While I didn't have a speaker phone, I took care that enough was communicated to ensure that everyone knew who I was talking to.

This is the Start of Something Beautiful

At some point in every negotiation I have been involved with in China, someone will suggest that this is the start of something beautiful: this is the beginning of a long and fruitful relationship.

This is a very Chinese approach to business: the Chinese do business with friends. There are many reasons for this, but perhaps one particular driver for this has been the lack of confidence in contract law and an absence of appeals to courts.

This may be changing as China develops the institutions of a modern economy, but it is still an important factor.

Getting access to products and getting introduced to people may be reliant on guanxi (pronounced "gwan-shee"—in highly simplistic terms, this is the Chinese concept of relationships), but once the introduction has been made, the meals eaten, some baijiu consumed, then in my experience it's all about money.

Typically, the further north you go in the country (towards Beijing), the greater the emphasis that is placed on guanxi. In Shanghai, because it is (and has historically been) a much more international city, the notion of suggesting that you might know a particular official who may have influence or can get you in somewhere, is far less likely to be mentioned than elsewhere in the country.

China has so many people coming to the country who are all looking to build relationships that it is common for Chinese companies to suggest "this is the start of something beautiful" to secure a good deal and then not even to invite the company to the next round of bidding on a project.

The notion of doing business with your "friends" normally translates in Chinglish to all other things being equal we will do business with the cheapest but pay lip-service to the notion of friends. I made a rule early on, after talking to many experienced people in the investment industry in China, never to sign up to something to get favorable treatment in a future negotiation as it would probably never happen.

Furthermore, I felt that the argument that this is the start of something beautiful would undermine the value we brought. I have even caught myself using this suggestion on some occasions to Westerners—I wasn't believed then either.

There is a second important point to this concept that is specific to China. Over six years of business in China I have experienced business relationships rise and sadly, fall. Each business relationship has a shelf life and follows four distinct phases.

- The first phase is the getting to know each other phase. This is characterized by lots of meals, rice wine, introductions to random third parties (the wife or daughter, for example), and uninvited visits. Like a prolonged first few days at school, an assessment is happening as to whether someone is qualified or useful to enter into a friendship or business relationship.

- The second phase is the most productive phase where both parties are working together in a constructive manner. Both parties are adding real value and are supporting each other in achieving their objectives.

- The third phase—which can often last for as long as half the relationship—is where one party starts to take advantage of the other party, often by introducing unrealistic demands. One party takes the other party for granted: perhaps they have the money in the bank and see little reason for cultivating the relationship going forward.

- The fourth and final phase is where one or both parties start acting dishonestly knowing that the relationship is over. Mercifully this is in normally the shortest phase as someone is getting burned.

In my experience, the critical issue is to understand when the third phase of a relationship starts and get out before the final phase. I know many people who have "lost it in China" and it has generally been because they entered into a long and beautiful business relationship that later entered the third phase and they incorrectly thought that the relationship could be rescued. The old maxim that once something starts to go wrong, it generally keeps going wrong is very true in China.

For the theorists, the perfect situation is if you can enter into a business relationship and make your exit at the exact point when it enters the third phase. However, this is rarely feasible in practice.

The Endurance Triathlon

Once down to business, the main form of Chinese negotiating tactic is usually the endurance triathlon which combines trial by sleep deprivation, trial by smoke inhalation, and trial by arduous consumption.

I came across this when I was negotiating with a lawyer over a group of large apartment blocks in the Xu Hui district of Shanghai, for us it was a comparatively small deal, but with property even small deals involve large sums of money and therefore intense negotiations.

The lawyer was obviously a friend of a friend of the chairman, and so he was directly hooked in to "Mr Big". This meant that this lawyer was able to overrule the manager of the development and so there were already very strange power dynamics in play when we got down to the negotiation.

I think it was during our second meeting that the lawyer threw his tea leaves at the "general manager" of the development and told him to "shut up".

We found the lawyer telling the general manager of the development to shut up on various occasions. Life in China has many absurdities, but negotiating contractual wording with an overpowering lawyer and a general manager who is picking Chinese tea leaves out of his clothing was certainly up there towards the top.

The lawyer had very long, slightly wavy, greasy hair, smoked Double Happiness cigarettes endlessly, and wore a suit with creases that suggested the possibility of him sleeping in the office. He carried three mobile phones that took turns to ring. He was obviously a well-regarded lawyer, and while at the time for me and my lawyer this individual appeared to be like a cartoon character, he was incredibly effective in achieving his goals.

For this particular lawyer his negotiating techniques were straight out of the school playground. He would regularly fill the room with smoke, swipe his tea onto the floor, and on one occasion he locked the door and said no one was going to leave until we had reached agreement. Rather than make a hostage plea to the embassy, I resolved to sit back and take in the entertainment.

At the time my Chinese was much weaker than it is now and I was able to watch the show without being troubled by the intricacies of the language. This enabled me to see this lawyer's performance for what it was—a well rehearsed act—rather than getting bogged down in the detail of what was being said.

The developer had many people on their team, but this lawyer had power over and above what a normal lawyer might be expected to have. He was the central artist where everyone else was just a supporting act.

Trial by Sleep Deprivation

I sat in on arguments/negotiations from 10 in the morning until gone midnight on several occasions. This was an occasion where a team of negotiators who can take it in turns was critical.

I never go into a negotiation in China with less than 3 people otherwise I feel there is a danger I could be eaten alive. For our negotiations, sometimes the other party had 10 people on their side of the table and they tried their best to wear us down on so many issues. To this day I have no idea of the roles of some of the people who have appeared in negotiation meetings. Generally, the more important the lead negotiator, the more "cardboard cut-outs" are required to accompany the discussion.

Trial by Smoke Inhalation

It is said that more than half of all the cigarettes consumed in the world are smoked in China and at times it has felt like those across the table were troubled by how low that percentage was. I do not smoke and the best decision I ever made was not to accept a cigarette although I feared it might be discourteous—Chinese cigarettes are much stronger than Western brands, and are so cheap that they are thrown around like candy.

I suspected that these negotiations were completed in a poorly ventilated room on purpose in order to smoke us out. Coughing during the negotiation, or requesting a change of atmosphere (one containing breathable air), would have been rude or a sign of weakness, and negotiating outside was never going to work in the middle of winter.

Trial by Smoke Inhalation is a discomforting tactic which I always found difficult to address, but it toughens you up. We had a smoker on our negotiating team at Shanghai Vision, a martyr to our cause but an essential element of our negotiating team.

Trial by Arduous Consumption

The final stage of this triathlon is the Chinese meal: Trial by Arduous Consumption.

I was always alarmed when a menu imprecisely described an item as meat, vegetable, or organ. As a relatively conservative eater, colorful Chinese food is not what I would go out of my way to eat. That is not to criticize Chinese food—there are many wonderful dishes for every pallet. However, I have sat at meals where crocodile, monkey, dog, cat, snake, eel, intestine, pigeon, duck's tongue, chicken's feet, snail, frogs, brain, giblets, slug, beetle, moth, and parts of creatures that look as if they are straight out of an extinct animals text book have been on show. You name it, and it has probably passed on a plate in front of me at some stage in a restaurant in China as part of the negotiating process.

The national sport in China is "eating". Every conceivable occasion is accompanied with a meal and the Chinese have a rich variety of tastes. On one occasion one of my staff and I had the pleasure of lunching with the portly head of one of China's banks in the Pudong district of Shanghai. We were hoping to negotiate better terms of finance and rightly thought a meal would help.

When the menu came it was passed to one of my staff who didn't get chance to open it before the head of the bank said "we will just have one of everything". Four hours and dozens of dishes later we headed home full of guilt about the "meal" we had just consumed less than 10% of.

Meals are often accompanied by large amounts of alcohol where the foreigner is released from his cage and is given centre stage to embarrass himself or herself. Baijiu is the commonest form of poison: it is a spirit-strength rice wine accompanied by a loud shout of "gan bei" (meaning "dry glass" or down it). It would be a cardinal sin to shout gan bei to someone and misinterpret this for cheers and watch them down it while you take a small sip.

It is common, particularly in southern parts of the Yangtze Delta, for the locals to be drinking from a separate bottle of baijiu that contains water while the foreigner is invited to gan bei one drink after another.

There are two things to note about this trial. First, it is generally meant to by friendly. My first real experience of this was with developers in the wealthy city of Wenzhou and it left me feeling that I was under attack. But this is wrong; the other side wanted to lower my inhibitions and to become friendly with everyone. I didn't do the deal in Wenzhou in the end (I think) but they certainly succeeded in lowering my inhibitions, so I am told. Second, it is often used as a tool to get people to discuss business when they're not thinking clearly.

Trial by Arduous Consumption Survival Strategies

Particularly with the Trial by Arduous Consumption, my strategy was to avoid the trials wherever possible and delegate them to my staff. I don't believe that the Chinese really enjoy them. In particular, the Trial by Arduous Consumption is done in the name of turning the foreigner into a circus animal. However, I do have several survival strategies that I use (and have seen used) to deal with the Trial by Arduous Consumption.

Have a Routine Prepared

I have experienced many meals with an old China hand from Australia who had worked out a routine for baijiu meetings which was hilarious.

He would whistle like a soccer referee and hold up red cards to the waiters, take bottles of beer and pretend to open them with his eye socket while providing the sound effects as others watched on in amazement, and sing Unchained Melody so that everyone in the restaurant and those outside could hear. His top party trick was to retreat to the toilet (Chinese dining rooms often have a private toilet for each table) where he would use the toilet roll to bandage his head and make an arm sling—he would then squash a tomato on his forehead before coming crashing out into the restaurant to laughs and applause.

Having acted the clown and become the subject of conversation for thousands of Chinese families, he always got the deal. A bit childish perhaps, but whatever works... and he avoided the harsh drinking while he was entertaining.

Trust Your Colleagues and Eat Less

I always brief my colleagues and have become an expert at chasing food around my plate. Where many foreigners will jump straight in and eat everything that is served, I am probably in the minority here and eat less.

I rarely went anywhere near some of the more extreme foods in China and my Chinese colleagues knew it. When we went to a restaurant they would make a dash for the menu and order on my behalf. I also ensure that my team is large enough to allow one person to remain sober if there is baijiu floating around. Having a driver attend the meal is a good way of guaranteeing this.

Chinese Negotiation: Price

The only thing I will guarantee in any negotiation in China is that the Chinese will generally think out how they are going to approach the interaction. Often a situation will start as a negotiation but will descend to a straight haggle.

A key factor about negotiation in China is that it tends to be much less sophisticated than in other markets because, in the vast majority of negotiations, there is normally only one thing that is important: the price. I have many examples of where other issues were not factored-in, allowing us to improve the deal because we knew before we entered the room that the person on the opposite side of the table probably had a very unsophisticated performance measure, and it was almost certainly the price.

For example on one deal we gave the seller an extra 1% to delay the payment—the interest saved by our investors was well above the 1%. On another we factored into the price a decoration budget which again was well above the additional cost. On one deal we set the price in Chinese RMB and then said we would deliver funds in USD and we would choose which of the official exchange rates to use (obviously the one in our favor).

This is the difference between negotiation and haggling. In haggling there is only one thing that is important (nearly always the price). By understanding that the other party would probably be measuring success on a crude indicator such as the price, we were regularly able to get other expenses and often work factored into this.

The Chinese are becoming more sophisticated, and as they open up are getting better at getting what they want. But until their performance measures become more sophisticated, the only issue that is likely to be important in a negotiation is price.

Chinese Negotiating Tools

I can only talk from the experience that I have had negotiating in China and so I cannot detail *every* negotiating tool that is in use. Equally, I cannot guarantee that any of these tools will be used, not least since different techniques can be applied in different industries. However, here are a few of the techniques that I have come up against.

Ulcer-Inducing Avoidance

Avoidance as a technique is used the world over, but it is far more powerful in China because few people ever write anything down and the Chinese seem to place less value on time than other nationalities. Even lawyers don't write things down—everything is done off the top of the head.

It might seem incredibly basic, but writing things down is important. However, the Chinese don't tend to do this. Perhaps this is because of the Chinese writing system which makes writing anything down more of an effort. Even well-educated people will not make lists. This makes avoidance an effective negotiating tactic because many issues are lost.

Whenever anybody says "let's come back to that", it is imperative to ensure that this is noted down. I knew if things were not noted I would find at a later stage that I had "agreed" to the point or it had been conveniently forgotten.

I have never sat in a negotiation where the other decision maker has had so much as a notebook to write things down. Sometimes they may have a junior member of staff note down a few points, but these would then be written in the back of a diary or even once a multi-million dollar contract was negotiated with the decision maker on the other side noting a couple of key points on the back of his hand. I spent most of the rest of the meeting watching as these notes then slowly rubbed off.

You Don't Understand China

"You don't understand China" is one of the most commonly used negotiating tactics. It is used to justify breathtakingly outrageous assertions—issues that nobody would ever agree to when doing business anywhere else in the world.

It would be inconceivable to say "I'll buy your house, but we won't have a contract... you don't understand America". That proposition would be laughable in the US and in most of the rest of the developed world.

Not only is this perhaps the most commonly used negotiation tactic, but it is probably the most pervasive, and can be heard in all industries. While the notion behind the concept may be reasonable—and I would encourage you to understand China before (and while) you do business there—in my experience this comment is always used in the most outrageous manner to justify the unjustifiable.

Here are some examples:

> ...we don't need a contract—you don't understand China

...breach clauses—only foreigners need breach clauses because they don't understand China

...definitions of the jurisdiction—you don't understand China

...you pay me everything up front, plus 10% and I won't have anything written down about what I am required to deliver—if you don't agree, you don't understand China

I have heard these in every negotiation I have ever sat in.

The argument can be an appeal to the stupid, an attempt to make you feel stupid, or a way to the change the subject and it works for most Chinese. As a foreigner it is difficult to say "yes I do understand China and what you are saying has nothing to do with China".

I have never resorted to the reverse of this argument—that "China doesn't understand foreigners", the right opportunity never presented itself—but I would wager it would not be taken seriously, so I didn't take this appeal seriously and was always able to either understand or get them to understand me.

Splitsies

We did business with many colorful characters, one of whom was Mr Gu.

Mr Gu has been in business about 20 years, which is a long time in China. He speaks fluent Japanese and is very close to the Japanese community. He is very intelligent and well connected.

He's got a trading company, a property management company, a development company, a food company, a clothing retail company, and several other unrelated businesses. It's an incredible conglomerate which is a mishmash of family-owned businesses merged together with Mr Gu at the center.

In many ways, he is the living embodiment of the Chinese entrepreneur.

He does a lot of entertaining and is particularly hopeless at golf. Indeed, he has worked on ensuring his performance at golf is good enough to merit a game, but bad enough to always be the runner up: it has never been in his interest, ever, to win a game of golf.

I negotiated endlessly with Mr Gu over every detail in the several deals we worked on together. Sometimes he was right, sometimes he was wrong, sometimes he was in a strong position, sometimes a weak position. Every time he employed the same negotiation trick: splitsies. Now this is not an uncommon technique around the world: you can't reach agreement, so you compromise and split the difference. Mr Gu entered every negotiation with us knowing that his aim was to steer the conversation towards splitting the difference.

He would encourage us to say our price, what time we wanted something, how high or how low, or how long or how short we wanted anything, and would then work out what he wanted and double it. His figure would then be double the difference so that when this is split you get back to the actual number he wanted all along. These discussions took many unnecessary hours resulting in a smile and an offer to split the difference. He would get what he wanted all along; either because we spoke first or his relentless questioning allowed him to calculate his position based on our strength or weakness on a position.

His weakness here was to repeat this tactic too often. While his first consideration was financial, he split everything else too: timing, delivery of payments, breach penalties, and so on.

There is an advantage about talking first as it allows you to place a stake in the ground. But since the splitsies game is played so frequently in China in my experience—both within the context of relationship building and as a negotiation tool—when I would pitch first, I knew that any first offer would be split at some point. It would be almost troubling if the counterparty accepted our first offer.

Wounded Pride: Street Slang

The wounded pride tactic is something that can be seen on many street corners throughout China. This is where a price is suggested that so offends the vendor that they may rock backwards into their seat, take in a sharp intake of breath, or press their hands against their chest in a manner that suggests they are about to have a heart attack at your appalling suggestion. Needless to say what you may have offered may have been the best price they had ever heard, but the Chinese DNA is programmed to feign offence at the first price.

With street negotiations, the secret is to play along. I have seen foreigners successfully describe themselves as a poor migrant farmer using the Shanghainese semi-sarcastic term "Mingong" and asking for the best price in Shanghainese slang ("bin ye in ge"). This will earn a smile and break the act.

These tactics are difficult to transfer from the street into the boardroom (though not impossible). However, knowing the native accent of who you are negotiating with is critical for breaking the tension. We negotiated with people from Guangzhou, Chong Qing, Shanghai, and probably China's richest province Zhejiang—each have very different accents, mannerisms, and approaches. I would often choose a junior member of staff to accompany us to negotiations if they were from a similar part of the country. The concept of a home town is very strong in China and having someone who spoke the home town dialect was often important.

Getting Past the Gatekeeper

There is a common form of negotiation where the negotiator is not empowered to make a deal. Instead, they are acting more as a gatekeeper to the person who has the power to make the deal. We came across this when negotiating in what was to become our first major deal.

We were negotiating to acquire a group of one- and two-bedroom serviced-apartments in a development located on the border of the two central districts of Shanghai: Jing An and Chang Ning. We were negotiating with probably the largest state-owned Chinese developer which is one of Asia's largest real estate development companies and had many meetings before we got the magic meeting with what appeared to be the real decision maker.

Ironically the policy of restricting access to the big boss was then used to not take any decisions. This meant that the boss could later disagree with what was said at the important meeting and hold back decisions for further negotiating advantage. As this was our first major deal we took just under a third of the building. I sensed that the terms were good and that this might work extremely well with our investors, so I included an option on the remainder of the building in the contract.

When the contracts were ready we took it to our investors who we had been priming for several weeks about the high-level terms. The investors loved the project and it was allocated to investors within hours. Inevitably we were desperate to get the remainder of the building but, possibly because we returned too quickly, the big boss simply disappeared and all of his minions disappeared too, fearing that they had given us too good a deal. With no decision maker available to confirm the additional areas of the building we wanted to take, our option could not be completed in time.

These sorts of negotiations are tricky. What I now do is take a laptop and a small portable printer so that the contract can be written, printed, and signed during the key meeting. The challenge is that you never quite know when this is going to happen; therefore a lightweight laptop is as essential as a watch in China.

While this filtering is quite frustrating, in many ways it's a natural consequence of how business is carried out in China where there are so many people. It is always worth reflecting that the numbers of people are staggering. For example, when we advertise for accounts people on a job web site, we might expect thousands of responses. In that type of environment, you need some filtering. Equally when trying to sell a product, it is certainly possible to be overwhelmed by interest, and so having filters is an inevitable consequence.

The lesson learned is that while decisions are theoretically taken at the top, in practice, many decisions are taken lower down the food chain, and the decision of giving access to the decision maker is an integral one to getting the deal. Again, a laptop and printer can help ensure that everyone's memory of an agreement made with a lower level functionary stays the same.

Not My Problem

When negotiating with representatives of the public sector it is common for the person on the other side of the table to have no vested interest in getting the best deal, or even an interest in any deal.

When dealing with the public sector, sometimes price and terms are not the motivating factor for the person who is involved in doing the deal: for them it will often be the hassle factor. They will want what allows them to take the least responsibility and have least accountability for their decisions. I think that this is an observation about the public sector the world over, of course. But given that China is growing out of a socialist economy where literally everyone once worked for the government in some way, this mentality is widespread.

These are hugely frustrating negotiations as your negotiating partner may have no vested interest in getting the best deal. It is even more frustrating when the person feels it is not in their interest to get any deal.

We had a situation where we decided quite late in the day not to go forward with a deal with a government developer. However, we found another company that was prepared to take the deal on and continue with the negotiation. I put this to the developer as a win/win/win situation: the developer got another potential buyer who may even pay more.

However, the developer had no interest in picking up on the deal. They had already decided to unwind the arrangements and had lost interest in making *any* deal. It was too much hassle, too much aggravation for the people involved.

The way to address this is often to understand the individual more. On our second deal, the government increased the requirements on notaries public working with foreign investors. Therefore we had to motivate notary public officials to work with us for the same money but a lot more work.

The answer came in taking the head of the notary public office out for dinner. I learned from him that his daughter had just finished school and was about to go university in Australia, but was worried about her level of English. I suggested that she come and work for us as a summer intern. For a couple of weeks I had a great summer intern which cost nothing more than a few meals, and the full cooperation from the notary public office.

Hotel Lobby Negotiations

Hotels are often designed with large lobbies with lots of private areas where meetings can take place. Often this is where alternative agendas—such as incentive payments—will be discussed. This, again, is true the world over.

We always avoided this sort of meeting but sometimes it is the only option. Contrary to popular belief, backhanders are not a prerequisite of doing business in China, particularly in the top tier cities. However, I always believed that negotiations that are arranged in hotel lobbies generally have alternative agendas above and beyond regular business.

To give an example of this, we once travelled to Nanjing to meet the owner of a building in Shanghai in a hotel lobby. The owner claimed that they didn't want to meet us in their offices because he didn't want his staff to know that he was considering selling the building. Yet at the same time he seemed to be in a hurry to sell. Our due diligence on the building later uncovered several illegal structures and a defect in title. The building was bought by a European group of investors several weeks later who may or may not know what they have bought.

I always prefer to avoid meetings in hotel lobbies, unless I am negotiating with someone who is staying in the hotel.

Deceit and Making It Up As You Go Along

In my experience, the Chinese relationship with the truth is different from the relationship that Westerners may have. In China it is often not frowned upon to say something that you know is not accurate—even outright lying is not frowned upon—if it is for the greater good, or what is perceived by the (deceitful) person as the greater good. In this context, the greater good may be the company, the country, or the family. The notion of the greater good is a comparatively fluid concept.

This is something that took a lot of getting used to. I have regularly done business with people who were—to my Western way of thinking—bare-faced liars. In China outcomes are far more important than the way they are reached. The truth and perceived truth will be sacrificed if a more positive outcome can be achieved.

The important thing I have found is to take little on face value and assess the credibility of all information.

Check It, and Then Re-Check It

The key to dealing with this attitude to the truth is to check everything and then to re-check it.

I always try to check everything using several sources and randomly check facts myself. I don't get upset when I discover that most of what I was told was absolute rubbish, intentionally misleading, or more commonly, a guess. People in China generally do not say "I don't know the answer to that" and instead, they guess. Therefore it is inevitable that there will be information that is wrong.

In fairness, Western values and conversation tend to be logical, but when we hear things we do not necessarily put them into the proper context of what has been said, the environment, the aggressiveness, or humility of the speaker.

Yes often doesn't mean yes in China. Generally the word yes means "I understand what you say". A classic logic difference in China: "Are you from Mars?" "Yes, the answer is no". This sentence makes perfect sense. But if you didn't hear "the answer is no", you may be left wondering who you really are doing business with. A more serious real world example might be "do I get my money back if you are in breach" being answered with "yes, no you don't".

Record Conversations

The practice of recording conversations is far more common in China than in most other countries and there is a common perception that a recording—even a hidden recording—is permissible evidence in court.

I'm not in favor of clandestine recordings since to pull out a hidden recording would be such an affront to the business face of the person that the only recourse would be to close down the business relationship. When I want to record something, I'm quite open about it and put the recorder clearly on the table. I then explain or make a bit of a joke about it, saying it will help me with my Chinese.

This immediately makes people a little bit more conscious about what they are saying and what they are promising. However, it won't necessarily make people adjust what they would say if they were under oath. I have some howling lies on record—sometimes I listen to old recordings when I am in a nostalgic mood.

Write Things Down

Be seen to write things down. The Chinese don't have anything such as shorthand and so they tend to make only the most basic of notes, if any. I always make sure that I am seen to be writing down actions and decisions in meetings so that my assistant can reply to the individual with an email detailing exactly any outcomes of a discussion.

Chinese people generally look at me as if I am stupid. I believe that it's better for them to think that and be wrong, than for me to miss something and for them to be right.

Take Business Cards or ID Numbers and the Manager's Name

People often lie to get out of doing a piece of work. For instance, it is common for bank clerks to say "it can't be done". If you look this up in your phrase book under the "at the bank" section "it can't be done" will probably translate to something like "I can't be bothered".

There is a mentality in China that exchanging money from RMB to another currency is stealing from China, irrespective of the official paperwork. Many Chinese people simply cannot believe that it is allowable to take money out of their country. Therefore cooperation when trying to do this is not always forthcoming.

A simple way around this is to ask for business cards or ID numbers and the manager's name. This has helped me overturn many routine transactions that "cannot" be done.

Imperialist Guilt

The imperialist guilt trip is played a lot less in Shanghai than it is in the Pearl River Delta around Guangzhou and up in the north around Beijing. Historically Shanghai has always been a highly international city and so the only time I heard it mentioned was in jest.

However, some business people are regularly told that all of China's problems relate to the short period of history when foreigners attacked China.

While foreign activity in China cannot be condoned, and in many cases was reprehensible, for many this attitude has become an urban myth that cannot be dispelled. The most straightforward approach to this attitude is to respond with flattery. You could even say "it is amazing how incredible the Chinese achievements have been since those dark days" and move on swiftly.

Zero Sum Negotiations

Every negotiation in China is a zero sum negotiation. In other words, if one party gets something, this is seen as a loss for the other. You win, I lose. This attitude may be tied in with face. The key issue here is to present yourself as being on the right side, in other words, the losing side.

In my experience Chinese companies do not really understand the concept of win/win negotiations. The capital that they tie up in face—irrespective of how much actual value they place on it—means that every inch lost is a bitter defeat.

The problem in negotiating is that everything essentially boils down to an inability to recognize gains and a bitter personal obsession with loss. The Chinese often think that everyone is out to get them and that everything is a struggle.

I used to employ the ten times rule. Every time I conceded something I would ensure I mentioned it ten times on ten different occasions. I would make a note of the ten times to ensure I did.

If there is ever a black and white case of I win you lose, then that is trouble. Sometimes I would have to think laterally to recognize victories I could credit to the opponent, however tenuous. Even getting me to come over to their office, agreeing to their choice of restaurant, or them wearing a smarter shirt than me, can be accredited as a victory.

The Tantrum

I have already mentioned the lawyer we dealt with in one particular negotiation. This was an individual who could really put on a show. We argued incessantly about lots and lots of the most trivial points on the contract. As well as smoking us out with his Double Happiness cigarettes in an unventilated room, he would negotiate well into the night—12 hour stretches with this lawyer were not uncommon.

On one occasion, after 10 hours arguing over the most trivial point imaginable he swept his Chinese tea off of the table and started to cry. He spent over two hours screaming in a high-pitched schoolgirl-like manner as if he were in the playground. Ultimately, when he hadn't got his way, he needed another technique and employed the tantrum.

In this case, he had invested so much in this one point, that he couldn't let it go. This meant that we had to give him something so that he could feel that he had a small victory that we would tell everybody about. The alternative was that we wouldn't move forward.

Unfortunately the relationship only got worse, so we had to seek out Mr Big (the owner of the company), and get him to plead with the lawyer. The boss had to tell the lawyer that he had done a great job but in the interests of getting the deal done, he should make the deal on the current terms as the risks weren't that great.

With hindsight this lawyer got a lot of what he wanted. He wasn't the best lawyer from a legal analysis/arguing in court perspective, but if I were to list the points that were open for negotiation, then his success rate was pretty high, and he achieved this by being so animated.

Strategies for the Outsider

While the Chinese may have some great haggling techniques, negotiation in China isn't a one way street. The deck isn't completely stacked against the outsider.

Here are some of the techniques that I have tried in my time in China.

Dumb Foreigner

There is a very successful approach that we have used in a number of our negotiations. A pre-requisite for this approach is a co-negotiator who is Chinese, and an incredible amount of trust between co-negotiators.

With this approach, we made sure that I appeared not to speak much Chinese. My Chinese co-negotiator then befriended the negotiator on the other side and would talk on a level that led them to believe that they were on their side. When sticky questions were asked my co-negotiator could then say:

> ...I can't translate that for the stupid foreigner, he will not understand...

> ...that will upset the foreigner; he is not intelligent enough to understand...

... it would embarrass you to ask such a complex question; let's keep it simple for the foreigner...

The Chinese are shockingly good at this level of duplicity.

The approach worked well as the person on the other side thought that they had an influence on the decision-making process while at the same time it allowed my side to steer the opponent towards items we wanted and away from decisions that we didn't want.

I have found this sort of selective translation is very successful as long as there is proper translation when the contract is ready.

I had a very well educated, very international, co-negotiator who went to the London School of Economics. We honed this style of me pretending to speak a lot less Chinese than I actually do and only taking cursory looks at contracts until they were ready. With each new negotiation we got better, and better, and better—it took literally dozens of hours out of the negotiations.

The approach allowed us to put a filter between us and the other person, and allowed the negotiator to refuse to translate certain points, or at least to discourage translation. The co-negotiator could pretend that they were closer to the other party and build a rapport using all the standard Chinese techniques such as flattery and ego massaging.

This raises another issue about whether to learn Chinese or not. There are as many people in Shanghai who have learned Chinese and regretted it as there are people who wish they could learn Chinese. Unquestionably, life in China is better and easier once a certain grasp of Chinese has been reached— the question is whether to take speaking Chinese into the workplace or the boardroom.

The difficulty with leaning Chinese is that you will never have the familiarity that native speakers have. By learning

Chinese and shouting about it, the filter you put between you and the person with whom you are doing business is gone. This filter allows me to control the pace of business and to take my time discussing certain points. Negotiating directly in Chinese is exceptionally difficult for all foreigners.

Show Me Some Face

I have always believed that the face issue is overplayed—money talks.

I always dislike using the face argument largely because, in my experience, I know that the Chinese will dismiss the concept of face immediately if they are put on the spot to defend it. But if there are small points to iron out, asking them to show a bit of face would roughly translate to showing some respect and just going along with the point.

I have found that this will only work on small points that cannot be easily traded.

Write the First Draft

The Chinese will never write a fair and balanced contract. To short-circuit the process of receiving something hopelessly one sided, I have always chosen to start the process myself. I write the first draft of the contract and make it hopelessly one sided: it has certainly saved me weeks or months of work.

The Killer Line

If all else fails, I have a killer line that has a 100% success rate in my experience. This line can be used in work or outside, but be careful, it cannot be used very often. Part of the success is the look on your colleagues' faces when you deliver this line: it is a notion that crosses cultures.

With Mr Gu we had been negotiating on a point in a contract on which he wanted to renege. The effect of his proposal was to change a guaranteed payment that we were required to pass to our investors. Given that this was a guaranteed, contractual payment, there was no room for any sort of change. This guarantee was how we raised the money and encouraged investors.

After a couple of weeks of negotiation on this point with Mr Gu, he came to our office rather than having us chasing him around town—he needed this point and was prepared to do anything to get it and therefore he wanted to show me a victory by going out of his way. I was losing patience—it seemed as if he was playing the endurance routine as well as giving me worthless victories to get his way (he rarely troubled himself to come to our office). He may even have had some form of split calculated in his head, but I was in no mood to accommodate anything on this key issue.

I had three of my colleagues in the meeting room, the head of our asset management arm, a senior investor manager, and a senior accountant: they knew that Mr Gu had huge reserves of stamina and was ready for a long negotiation. I walked around the meeting table, sat next to him—abnormally close—I leaned over and said "do you understand the damage you are doing to our relationship?"

The reaction of my colleagues could not be faked. They were genuinely shocked. Mr Gu's assistant stumbled to translate, but the effect was perfect. He excused himself from the meeting and capitulated by the end of the day.

The reaction of my colleagues and the fact that it was totally out of character had added to the impact of the line, and in China this has a big effect. I don't subscribe to the concept of face in China, but to challenge someone on their "relationship" that will have been cultivated, boasted about, and managed over months of meetings and meals is to land a punch squarely.

I would suggest that this line can only be used with any one person and with any one group of witnesses. But it works.

Lessons Learned

Here are some of the main lessons I have learned during my time haggling in China.

- When you come to the negotiation table, always remember that the most important thing for the Chinese person is probably just the price, and money is often the only measure of a deal.

- Ensure you are talking to the decision maker, write everything down, and check everything twice.

- Have reserves of stamina, patience, and snacks for negotiation. This is not going to be quick...

- Ensure you have alternatives, and ensure the other party knows you have alternatives.

- It is something of a universal truth, but one that is still very valid in China: if you are selling you need to strip everything out of the price that you can, but if you are buying you need to add into the price everything you can.

- Never do a deal that you wouldn't do on the same terms anywhere else in the world.

- Friendships, relationships, and contracts evolve and have a life cycle. Retain some power or control at every stage of that cycle.

- Prepare to negotiate in China, not in a Western environment. Keep your sense of humor, patience, and killer line ready and you'll be fine!!

Chapter 5

Everybody's Number One Challenge: Human Resources

Bob Boyce could have followed the family business and become a rancher in his home State of Montana. But instead, upon graduating, Bob saw the US economy was not in great shape and seized an opportunity to study Chinese in Beijing. After finishing his studies in China, he gave himself a month to find a job—he found one on the second day and hasn't looked back since.

Bob's first restaurant was started because it was difficult to find straightforward, casual Western food at a reasonable price. By chance his room mate at the time worked in the restaurant business in Guangzhou, southern China. The two decided to give the food and beverage business a shot together. The first restaurant opened in 1999—there are now 11 (with three new venues scheduled to open in 2009) and the company currently employs over 600 people (and that figure is rising quickly).

Having got the concept right, the "blue frog" formula has been repeated. A focus on the formula, coupled with flexibility to meet the needs of the clientele in each location, has provided a solid business model for the company. By adopting what Bob calls "family-style management," the group has gone from 200% turnover rates to having one of the lowest turnovers in the industry, averaging less than 13% each year. This low turnover has been a crucial factor in creating the environment for the company to grow.

In this chapter Bob talks about his experiences overcoming the number one challenge within Chinese businesses: people.

During our first year, we built up a really successful business. The first restaurant was on Maoming Road, a bar street that later became synonymous with entertainment and going out in Shanghai.

About a month after opening our second restaurant, my partner told me that she wanted out of the business, so we worked out a deal and I bought her share of the company. Part of the buy-out agreement was that a loan from her family be repaid. This really changed my attitude to business as it was the first time I came up against the favors and relationship supporting arrangements that can sometimes be expected to complete deals in China. I had a huge loan to pay (made bigger as I borrowed to buy my partner out), two restaurants to handle, and 200% staff turnover.

I had three choices:

■ Run away.

■ Stay with two restaurants and send myself to an early grave.

■ Go for growth.

I chose option three. It quickly became clear that I was going to need to change the way I was running the company. I realized that I was not paying much attention to the people in my company. I was expecting them to come in and be committed to their jobs and to the company, but in return I wasn't reciprocating. I wasn't giving them anything more than a pay check. They had no reason to engage their futures with me or the company.

It was clear that the only way I could achieve growth was through building a much stronger team of people, so. I began to focus on what that team should look like. While strengthening the team, I also had to go back and really clearly define what the business was about. Getting the fundamentals right in the beginning helped a great deal in building a stronger team. With strong fundamentals, our people were much clearer about why they were working with us.

Business Fundamentals

The fundamentals of the business—our core—have always been the same. We've built our reputation on four simple principles:

- Great customer experience.

- Quality food and drink.

- Comfortable atmosphere.

- Reasonable prices.

Those four principles are what we always return to when we're looking at the menu or if we're considering a new venue. We've always had the fundamentals right. In my mind—in the way I envisaged the company—I have always been very clear about what I want, and what I want for the company. The fundamentals have not changed since we first opened and are the foundation upon which we've built the business.

From the beginning, we defined our core market as the white collar professional, irrespective of their ethnicity. After all, for me, Shanghai is about people living an international lifestyle in a global city. We have never been an ex-pat place or a Chinese place. We have always worked at creating and sustaining an environment where a modern international person can feel comfortable.

In the beginning most of our customers were foreigners because they were the people who most identified with what we were doing. At that time not many Chinese people had been in a Western bar or restaurant outside of a hotel. It took a while to get the word out and build a local customer base. As more locals started to travel, and to work in multinational companies, they started to identify more with what we were offering.

When we opened our first blue frog in the suburbs of Shanghai, it became clear that we were going to need to adapt what we were doing to the neighborhood. Many of our early customers had moved out to the suburbs and started families. We found that they still identified with what we had to offer but needed some changes in order to accommodate their kids. Pram (stroller) parking and a play area become really important to this blue frog.

From that experience we began to tailor each restaurant to the community we were in. The venues that are in suburban areas with a lot of families were made kid- and family-friendly. On the flip side, the blue frogs in the city locations are more adult-focused and may not be the sort of place that you would find kids each day. We strive to provide a setting that is a reflection of the neighborhood we're in.

The Necessity to Focus on People

There are a lot of people to employ in China, but skilled individuals with a depth of experience are harder to come by and to keep.

I think virtually anyone doing business in China has had challenges with recruiting and retaining good people. High turnover has become an accepted liability of doing business. Many companies complain about losing people to a competitor for a couple of hundred RMB more a month. In our industry, high turnover is an accepted—if much complained about—norm. For me, it was clear that the approach to just accept high turnover was not going to work. We had 200% turnover at one point—a ludicrous figure. Instead of complaining about it, I started to look at ways to build a better team and then keep them.

While it may sound clichéd, we are a people business—it doesn't get much more personal than providing people with food and drink. For us to be successful, we need our staff to be able to deliver a great experience to our customers. I don't believe they can do that if they themselves do not feel like they are working in a positive environment where they are valued.

Knowing that our people represent the face of the company each day, we recognized the need to work hard to teach our standards, share knowledge freely, and give our people the experience required to be successful when representing the company. We have always seen people as an asset, not simply a business cost.

One of the reasons we are able to keep our staff onboard with us now is by growing. If someone leaves the organization, they are losing an opportunity to move up in the company. We need good people to develop their skills quickly so we can get them moved into leadership roles. Adopting a growth strategy put our people at the heart of every move we have made.

Initial Recruitment Strategy

Our initial recruitment strategy, when the business first started, was to look for people with lower wage aspirations. We expected to try and save labor costs while developing skills on the job. We would hire anybody who could speak a little English and who had any experience.

This hiring approach changed very quickly as we realized the effort associated with trying to change attitudes, values, and previous work habits. We learned early on that hiring people with experience but with a bad attitude was a route to unhappiness. We learned that experience in China is difficult to quantify and easy to exaggerate. Just because someone has experience on paper doesn't mean that they can actually deliver, so we made a point of hiring for attitude and then teaching everything else.

In the beginning, we were never particularly scientific about finding the right attitude, especially in the early days—if they had a spark in their eyes, with a "get-up-and-go" attitude and good personal presentation, we would hire them.

In those early days, the whole human resource issue was a real challenge. Trying to figure out what made young Chinese people tick was really difficult and I wasn't ready for that. We ran the show like a mom-and-pop operation—we didn't have contracts or clear rules and there wasn't a lot of stability.

The Scale of the Challenge

In the first couple weeks of running what was to become the blue frog, a customer called me over to have a look at his food. He had ordered a beef burrito and inside was beef, as you would expect, and also cabbage. Our burritos weren't supposed to have cabbage in them so I apologized and marched the plate to the kitchen to find out what had happened.

The cook looked at the dish and asked me what was wrong. I pointed out there was cabbage in the burrito and asked why. It turned out that we were out of cheese and because he thought cabbage looked the same as cheese he assumed it would be just as good to use in the dish. The cook could see nothing wrong: he didn't understand the nuances of the flavor interactions.

It became clear that training was going to be key to the success of the business. There were not many Western restaurants in Shanghai in those days and there were few experienced staff. Those who did have experience were either trained in a hotel or a Chinese restaurant.

Most of our employees had never even eaten in a restaurant, let alone served Western food. We had to train them from the basics of how to eat Western food (including how to hold a knife and fork, which can be as difficult as using chopsticks for the non-chopstick user), all the way through to how to serve.

So began a long journey of standardizing recipes and training.

Retention

Once we trained people, it became hard to keep them because every place in town was looking for experienced people.

Three days before what would be one of the busiest weekends of the year, the week when everyone returns from summer holidays, my chef announced that he was going to be leaving for a different job. I took a deep breath and asked where he was going. He told me that the US Consulate General's wife had approached him about being her personal chef. I remember meeting her several weeks before in the restaurant. She had said she enjoyed the food...

I asked him when he was leaving and he told me that he was going in three days because she was having a big party at the Consulate and needed him to cook for the event. On his last day, three other kitchen staff resigned with no notice. Unfortunately for us, our payday was that week. The staff collected their checks and left us scrambling to keep up with the workload.

That weekend, the weather was great and our business took off. We had a full restaurant with three new cooks in the kitchen. It was the first really busy day of that year.

I spent the time running food and apologizing to customers while my manager at the time took over in the kitchen and my business partner tended the bar. We had a lot of customers who waited almost an hour for their food. I spent all of my energy explaining the situation to each customer, most of whom understood. People were a lot more forgiving in those days because they were just happy to have a place to go.

After that challenge, I reflected a great deal on how and why we got to a point where our staff would so easily walk away from the company. Since then, we've nearly mastered the art of documenting standards and recipes, and talent reviews across the company. We have constantly focused on building loyalty to the company, the opportunities at hand, and not tying the company's success to any one individual. Our growth strategies today support the successful promotion of colleagues across the company whenever the business need arises.

Through training and coaching we are always preparing staff to step up and successfully take on more responsibility. We've grown the business around community values, career development, and employee benefits, creating a culture of opportunity.

The Big Change: Laying the Foundations for Growth

The first years with the first two restaurants were quite chaotic. It was only when my business partner left that I really started to take things seriously: that was the point at which I grew up and recognized that the success of the company was on my shoulders. I realized I couldn't run the company alone and that meant I needed to change how I behaved. Everyone looked to me for the tough decisions, the final call, and the representation of company values. The buck stopped with me.

The early years were a journey of understanding what my strengths and weaknesses were (and are). I now understand that my strengths are not in administration and never will be. My strength is in setting the direction, growing the business, and leading people—being out front as the coach and cheerleader.

Understanding the depths of my strengths and my role in the company was a long process, but it was the beginning of a journey that gave me clarity on how to survive in an incredibly brutal market where restaurants come and go throughout the month. I had to learn to hire for the skills that I was missing, complimenting my strengths and bringing more experience to the company.

Hiring an administrative manager to look after employee contracts as well as general documentation like lease agreements and contracts with suppliers was the first step in setting me free from administration. Hiring a great accountant was the next move. If anyone asks me what I would do differently if I could do it over again, the answer is always that I would have hired a much better accountant at a much earlier stage.

Introducing Family-Style Management

After my partner left, I sat down and began a long conversation with myself about how to make the business work. Part of that thought process was to consider:

- Who are my people?

- What do I need from them?

- What do they need from the company and me?

- How do we create an environment where people want to stay?

At the time, most of the people in the company were under the age of 25 and had very little life or work experience. They were coming from homes where their parents grew up during the Cultural Revolution, where the government was the parent, the visionary, the employer, and the caregiver. Most of my people had very little guidance in their lives especially when it came to work and most of their parents had no idea what type of world their children were working in.

I asked myself what these people needed to get ahead, to create a livelihood of their own. In my view, people need clarity, stability, guidance, opportunity, discipline, and belonging. These are the things that a family provides, and that I wanted to provide for my employees in the same way. Because the family institution and belonging to a community are concepts that the Chinese relate to in a very real way, I established family-style management.

Almost overnight, I became an uncle, father, mother, older brother, coach, and disciplinarian to a growing number of eager young folks finding their way in the very new world of free markets, employers, and independent businesses. We were hiring people who were coming to us from all over China. These were kids coming into a world that they really had no idea how to deal with. China had changed so much in the previous 10 years that the world they were stepping into was one entirely different from that of their parents' generation. There really wasn't a lot of experience from which they could draw. We had to help them make the transition from sheltered home life into the working world in a way that worked and in a way that they were comfortable with.

Building the Business

Running a restaurant is a bit like having children: you can cope with two by holding onto one with each hand, but three is much harder. With two venues, you can run the business without processes so long as you are present constantly. When you reach three venues, you need the processes in place to ensure they run successfully, the way you want them run, when you're not around.

I love to build the business—that's my passion, but it's also a way of keeping our staff. As long as we're growing, our people will have a place to develop themselves and gain skills that they can use for the rest of their lives, in any company or endeavor they choose to take on. If young people don't have ambition, goals, or aspirations, then they're going to be unlikely to help grow the business.

Growth became a part of our strategy for managing our people, and promotion has been an integral part of keeping people. Of the senior management team today, we're probably split 50/50 between people who have worked their way from the ground up and those who we have hired in.

A good example is my executive chef who started with me eight years ago. He was in charge of six or seven people in the kitchen and now he's the executive chef in charge of 11 venues and 240 people. He has grown up with me. In his own words, "In the beginning I stayed because I could see that this guy (me) really needed help; now I stay because I can see the great company that we are creating together".

My training manager Sisi is in a similar situation. She is one of the pioneers in the company: a girl who got off a train from the middle of southwestern China, not really knowing what to expect.

We couldn't have said at the time that she would progress so quickly. She decided to embrace the challenge, try new things with us, and has, through hard work and determination of her own, progressed from running food to customer tables to Supervisor, Assistant Manager, Restaurant Manager, and now Training Manager for China. She stuck with it and worked hard and smart, and now she's responsible for the development and training strategy for over 600 people.

These are not the only examples: we now have a significant number of young people who started at entry-level jobs and, through working smart, are now managers earning more then most of their contemporaries in office jobs. Being able to offer our people the opportunity to move up has been a key factor in keeping great people in the company.

Introducing Clarity

When the business had two principals, we got along well, but we had differing (and sometimes conflicting) approaches to how we did business and how we would treat people in the business. Sometimes that difference would be confusing for people.

I learned that in the work place, people need clarity. They need to know where they stand and where they're going. People need to know what the rules are and what is expected in order to move up, to grow, and to ensure their own futures with the company. To address this, we put together clear contracts along with an employee handbook with our rules and code of conduct. All employees were required to read and sign the handbook—this took the guess work out of which set of values were right each day. Everyone in the company knew where they stood and was clear about the rules.

One comment that has always frustrated me is "maybe you don't understand this is how we do it in China." Having heard this over and over, my response is always the same: "I understand that that is how things might normally be done in China, but this is my company, and this is how we're going to do it. If you've got suggestions, then please let me have them. If they're good ideas, then we'll work with them, but at the end of the day, this is my domain, so we'll do things my way." The "my" in that statement has changed to "our" over the years. We have our own way of doing things and we require our people to be on-board with that way.

If the rules are clear, if the labor contracts are clear, and if the rules of engagement are clear, then our people tend to be more comfortable, and keeping consistency and discipline is a lot easier.

Belonging

Many of our people are working far from their home towns. They are a long way from home working in very large cities. This can be a lonely experience for anyone.

In the early days, everyone knew each other and so it was easy to establish a sense of community. I knew everyone by name and they knew me well. The strong sense of community back then helped solidify a wonderful company culture. We organized monthly outings for each venue's staff. We would give each venue a budget and let them use it in some fun way. The only rules for the gathering were that they all go together and the manager joins.

The opportunity to relax in a non-work environment really broke down barriers and helped create an environment of belonging for our people. That sense of belonging has contributed in a big way to lowering our staff turnover.

Those monthly gatherings have developed into community events organized by the employees themselves, but with company support. We've done beach parties, picnics, go-karting, and, of course, karaoke contests. We also have an active bicycle and soccer team. A strong community has led to reduced turnover because people don't want to leave their friends and their support network.

Standardization

We needed to standardize what we were doing for so many reasons:

- **Consistency.** We needed consistency between restaurants and even within the same restaurant. People want to know what they're eating and want to order what they like, and without consistency that doesn't happen. As we grew, our customers expected us to keep the experience consistent between venues. To this day our customers keep us honest about the amount of sour cream on one plate of nachos to the next and our ability to deliver the perfect Montana Burger regardless of location.

- **Focus.** We always knew what we did and understood what type of restaurant we were. It's incredibly important to stay true to who we are and what we enjoy delivering to the community. I had a chef who had a hard time following our recipes for classic American comfort food. We used to butt heads often because he wanted to do his own thing while I was trying to standardize recipes across multiple venues. He didn't like the food we were serving—he wanted us to serve classic French food because that was his background, but we weren't a French restaurant. We didn't have the same focus.

- **Knowledge.** The same chef who wanted us to serve classic French food had memorized all of our recipes (many of which he had said he didn't like). He didn't have them written down in any detail and I didn't insist that he did. When he left, the business was put in danger because the new chef was not able to immediately replicate these recipes, as they were not documented properly anywhere else. It became clear that we were going to need to become almost religious about standardized recipes and then training around those recipes. Some months after we parted ways he became the chef of a restaurant down the street with an exact knock off of our menu... So much for not liking American food.

Recruiting and Training

When we hire people, we need them to really buy into our core values and business philosophy because they're building a career with us and representing who we are to the community. This means we have to recruit the right people and then make sure the training is there to support their development and the consistent delivery of the customer experience that we promise to our guests.

Finding the right people has always been difficult. This was particularly so in the early days, but even today, our people are coming in from all over China and their experience of Western food is usually limited.

That generally meant that we had to train from absolute zero. As a young company, that was a really painful process, but it also was quite rewarding because we have been able to see people develop their skills, and have had a part in developing their future professional careers.

Before training, though, we have developed an interview process to ensure we find the right people.

Initial Interviews

We've spent a lot of time working on our initial recruitment process. That work has paid off with a reduction in bad or wrong hires.

The process is pretty simple. We start with the screening process. If someone has jumped jobs every year or in some cases every couple of months, we don't even interview them. No matter what they may say in the interview, our experience has shown that in our industry if they have job-hopped in the past, they will continue to do so. So we don't waste our time.

We then give the candidates a screening interview to make sure they actually have the experience that is outlined on their resume. It is amazing how many people fabricate their work histories. Usually simple questions about the position they say they held can determine whether they are on the level.

After the initial screening with Human Resources, they move into interviews with their future manager.

Much of the focus of this interview is on problem solving, so we ask them to tell us about challenges they have faced and explain how they met them. We have developed a standard set of questions for each position so that our interviews are consistent. We also like to ask detailed and technical questions if they claim to have experience in the restaurant trade as this highlights the depth (or otherwise) of their experience. If they are interviewing for a kitchen position we will put them in the kitchen and test their cooking skills.

During the interview process, we look at how interested and engaged the candidate is. If they have a good attitude and show an eagerness to learn, we look at them a lot more closely: no matter how much experience a person may have you cannot train a bad attitude. We also look at how much energy they have. If they seem lethargic and non-responsive, we don't give them much time.

The last part of the interview process is to check references and former employers. It still amazes me how many companies don't do this.

Just recently, we had a former employee try to pass himself off to another company as a star supervisor. We had fired him just a couple of months before for breaking and entering into the restaurant and stealing several thousand-RMB-worth of products and vouchers. He had been out of jail for about a week when we received a call from a friend at a well known restaurant in town checking this candidate's reference. It came as quite a surprise when we told him that our "star" supervisor had just been let go for theft.

All of this is not ground breaking stuff, but being methodical about the process has helped us a great deal in bringing on great people and keeping them.

Training

If we offer someone a job at a junior level, the first thing they will do is go through the training process. The training process is now based on our standard operating procedures (SOPs). We have SOPs for everything and getting the SOPs has been a long, painful process.

We have a permanent training department with two full-time trainers who have been with us for a long time. They walk our new recruits through our background and then I go in and talk about our core values—why they're important, why we have them, how they can use them—and we also talk about the philosophy of the company.

Once people understand the background and the philosophy of the company, the technical training for their position starts. If they're going to work in the kitchen, we start with food safety, hygiene basics, and step-by-step procedures to move raw ingredients from the supplier delivery to a beautifully-presented salad, prepared according to our standard recipe.

If they're going to work in the front of the house, we start with restaurant safety, hygiene basics, and step-by-step procedures to deliver our customer experience to each table. We give people a certain amount of training and then put them into the venues with a buddy whom they will shadow for at least a couple of weeks until they are ready to interact with our guests on their own.

We are careful to ease people in step-by-step. As a customer, there's nothing worse than being waited on by waiting staff who don't know what they're doing and can't figure anything out. The first step in our core values is to create a great customer experience. Bumbling staff don't create that great experience so we try not to let it happen.

We have a similar process in the kitchen. We put in the new recruit and start them cutting up vegetables, the same vegetables every day until they can prove they get the cuts right 90% of the time and then move them on to a wider variety of skills, such as dicing chicken or grilling salmon, testing their abilities, and providing certification for their advancement until they move from Kitchen Help to Senior Cooks over time. We work with them step-by-step as they grow.

Pay for Talent

One of the decisions we made early on is to pay our managers manager salaries.

We don't pay ex-pats more because they're ex-pats. We pay people based on their experience and what they bring. So if a local manager has more experience than non-local manager, then the local manager is going to earn more than the foreign manager.

That is something that has been really important to our growth. I can't justify paying somebody more just because they grew up somewhere else. The only way I can justify paying more is if the ex-pat has something to offer that I can't get locally.

An ex-pat may have a depth of experience that a younger Chinese person will not have, but that doesn't mean that the Chinese person can't get that experience—it's simply that they don't have it at the moment. Some people who have been with me for a while now have a lot of experience because we have been through everything together.

Identifying People to Progress

We need people to grow and progress so that we can grow the business. However, we need to make sure that we progress the right people.

One way we decide which people to progress is by testing. We test people for their knowledge of service and their knowledge of their job. In order for someone to move up a level, they have to pass a test. The testing is the first part of the progress, and if we are still thinking about moving a person up, we then interview them.

The interview is a hard core interview and weeds out a lot of people, but it also identifies people who are hungry to progress within the company. Those are the people that we invest in: I don't like to invest in people who won't improve themselves.

When we select someone to progress, we then work with them to make sure they get the necessary training. For us, progress is a very gradual step-by-step process.

We've made a lot of mistakes—promoting people too soon or too far, or promoting people who showed a lot of promise or who promised a lot and then didn't deliver. There have been a lot of mistakes along the way. However, with this test and interview process, we're getting much better at developing the right people.

Making the Leap from Staff to Management

The leap from staff to management is a long and painful process. This first jump is one of the most difficult jumps for anyone to make and this difficulty is the same in China as it is in the West.

For us, the biggest leap is from waiting staff to shift supervisor. Suddenly, you are a manager and no longer a co-worker. You have to get people to do what you want and need them to do or else you get into trouble—or so the belief among new supervisors often goes. The other person doesn't get into trouble—you do. It's a big lesson and a hard lesson for almost everybody, moving from what was a friendly relationship to a relationship of authority and responsibility.

We work hard to help people with and through this transition. We learned from the beginning that it's important to move people up slowly—we made some really good kids who were excellent waiters and waitresses into really bad managers and really bad employees because we didn't move them up slowly enough. They thought they were ready, they said they were ready—they were ready for the pay check, they were ready for the name card—but when it came down to it, they weren't ready to take the responsibility that comes with the title and the job.

While the first step from staff to management is a problem that is applicable around the world, there are some China-specific cultural issues. One issue that is highly significant in China is age. In traditional Chinese society, younger people give older people respect. For a young person to have to tell an older person what to do is culturally quite difficult, even if the younger person is at a senior level within the company. Culturally, the older person should be in charge.

There is also an issue about people taking responsibility. In the West, it is perceived as a good thing to have more responsibility and people will seek to take on more responsibility. For many Chinese, there is no cultural conditioning to take on responsibility in this manner, so it can be very difficult for people to accept their new accountabilities.

Very often people will take on their new role and when things don't happen they will say, "I told them to do it." It takes a long time until they understand that giving out orders is not enough (and, in any case, is simply not appropriate)— the role of supervisor is to ensure that something is achieved through consistent and reliable procedures, through coaching, training, and guidance—not through orders alone.

After losing a number of people because they just couldn't handle the responsibility or the pressure so quickly, we created different layers, or multiple steps to go up in management. We have two levels of Shift Leader, two levels of Supervisor, and four levels of restaurant management. This allows us to move people up gradually and gives them a chance to acclimatize to the change.

The market changes so quickly in China; in particular, salaries go up so quickly that if you make someone who is good wait a year to progress, they will have had ten offers while they wait and so the ability to offer many small steps helps us address that challenge.

People in our company can get promoted at any time throughout the year. We also have a company-wide annual review that allows us to assess the talent pool and further ensure consistency in our reward and career progression.

Logistical Challenges with a Growing Business

Growth as a concept is easy. Growth in its practical implementation is tough—even after you have laid solid foundations.

Going National

The logistics of having something going on in Macao while something else is going on in Beijing, and a whole bunch more is going on in Shanghai is quite a challenge. I love this business and I love all the venues—and I love being in all of them—so for me, one of the hardest parts is not being in my venues, with our people, especially at the moment when I'm setting up a new venue, which means I'm devoting all of my time and energy to the new venue and I'm not able to spend quality time with more of our staff across the region.

The challenge of making things work while I'm not with our people in person all the time is a big challenge. As I've beefed up the management team, I've got some great people with some great experience and I trust these people. Because I trust them, and because this is the way to grow, I've been able to pass the torch for operations to the team. That has been one of the big things that I've had to do to be able to open the business in multiple cities. There is a point at which the business *cannot* grow any more in a healthy way unless the person behind it gives up control and trusts people. We have passed that point.

I trust the management team's decisions—they're not always the decisions that I would make—but usually they're as good, or better, than the decisions that I would have made. If they're not, then we talk about it and we learn together. We learn from each other by a very clear and open discussion, and we go on. As a person, I'm quite direct, and as a company, we value directness, and open and honest communication. We can all butt heads and walk away from a very direct conversation knowing that everyone around the table has the best interests of the company at heart.

Learning about People: Gaining Some Perspective

When I first came to China as a student, I spent a lot of time traveling around the country. That was a huge help to me, and gave me a deep and detailed knowledge that was important when building the business.

You can't understand China if you just go to Shanghai and Beijing. Even after 15 years in the country there are lot of things I don't get and there probably will always be many areas which are closed to me and to most foreigners. I would say, however, that I understand a lot more about why things are the way they are after seeing how incredibly diverse the country is.

When I was a student in the early nineties I spent a lot of time traveling. I didn't have much money so I traveled like everyone else... on buses, trains, boats, and a few donkey carts. Spending that time seeing the country by the seat of my pants has helped me a great deal in understanding my people. Because I've been to a lot of the places they are from it's a little easier to connect with them and to understand where they are coming from. I relate to my staff differently—and probably on a deeper level—because of the time I spent traveling.

We have over 12 people in the company who can't read or write. There's not much we can do about that (though we have offered to help with classes)—you can't easily teach an adult how to read and write, and they're probably not that interested in learning anyway. But those same people are making sure that their kids are going to school. They are working incredibly hard at building a better life for the next generation.

I have a great example: a kitchen helper who started with us as a dishwasher. She was a young woman from Sichuan who was a pretty rough-around-the-edges individual from the country. She doesn't read or write, but she's putting her kids through school and she has worked her way up in the kitchen. She makes a good salary, which she sends home. Over the years she's bought property in her home village, so much so that she is now a big potato back there: she's a landlord. The power of that is profound and it makes me smile every time I think about it.

This woman came to Shanghai with nothing, worked hard, saved her money, and now she is building a better future. That is China's version of the American Dream.

Mistakes

While we've grown, and I'm hugely proud of what we have all achieved, I have made a lot of mistakes along the way. Too many, in fact, to list here in their entirety but the following are some of the big ones.

Administration

Early on the accounting was terrible. I was completely in the dark about accounting and how to run the nuts and bolts of my business.

In the early days I wasn't as engaged in the business part of the business. I was more engaged with my customers rather than dealing with the fundamentals of the business. It took a while for me to understand that I really needed to dig into this stuff.

That digging helped me to understand what I was good at and what I wasn't good at. However, the things I wasn't good at still needed to be done: it wasn't enough to take the attitude that I'm not good at something so I won't do it. Instead, I had to acknowledge that I wasn't good at it and figure out how to get things done until I could hire someone who could do it. That took a long time to figure out.

Patience

Patience has always been a big issue for me—I didn't always have patience and I am probably not always the most patient person. I've had to learn to take a deep breath, give people a chance, work with them, and give them an opportunity to make mistakes. The end result of letting people make mistakes is that they usually come out of a situation with more experience and a better understanding of the problem. Now if they repeat the same mistakes too frequently, then there is probably a problem.

Probably the most important thing that I've learned while in China is that it takes patience and perseverance to make things work. You have to figure out how to go forward. Sometimes it doesn't work and sometimes you've got to listen to how it's always been done, and then you've got to work it that way. Sometimes you've got to listen to how it's always been done and then do it a different way. Part of being successful in China is working out what to do when there is a wall in your way.

I've needed to be persistent: there's almost always a way to get around, or over, most barriers in China, as long as you are determined, and willing to explore different routes and avenues (including the occasional tree climb or cliff dive). That was a big lesson for me and it took a long time to get.

Lessons Learned

- Take the time to understand people (wherever they come from) and get to grips with the Chinese culture as best you can—even if only so that you can understand when you are doing something that your people may find uncomfortable.

- Hire great people. If you are training people, then enthusiasm counts far more than untested claims of experience that may be coupled with a poor attitude. Once you've got great people, then good processes will help these people succeed.

- When you've hired a great person, keep them. Build a business that gives everyone the space to be able to grow. Make sure that you give them more options than to grow out of your door.

- Get the processes right and then grow—not the other way round.

- Have a deep understanding about what's going on in your business and what really matters. There are so many undercurrents that you may not be aware of due to language and culture, and if you don't pay attention to the details, then other people may take advantage.

- Confirm your focus and the foundations that will always support your business, be 100% clear about what you aim to achieve, and then gather your people and get them involved in the purpose. You will be amazed at what can be accomplished, regardless of the challenges presented, when your people are included in the journey of creating something great.

Chapter 6

Fostering Creativity in China

Montgomery Singman (Monte) is the founder and CEO of Radiance Digital Entertainment, a Shanghai based online game producer and publisher that now employs over 100 people in Shanghai.

Monte is a veteran of the US video game industry, having participated in the production of John Madden Football, Test Drive Off-Road series, Street Fighter series, Looney Tunes Racing, and Soviet Strike, among others.

He was the founder and CEO of Zona—a middleware company supporting the massive multiplayer online games industry—which was acquired by Shanda Entertainment in 2003.

In addition to his busy work schedule, Monte is also the chief professor at Shanghai Theatre Academy heading the digital entertainment school. He is the author of several books in Chinese on the subject of creativity and next generation online gaming.

In this chapter Monte looks at the challenges of finding the creativity in people who have been indoctrinated for generations with Confucian conformity and where creativity has been systematically removed over the last two generations.

143

My father was an American who went to Taiwan in the 1960s where he met and married my mother. After the wedding they stayed in Taiwan, and I was born and raised in the country. I didn't speak English until I left Taiwan in 1989 at the age of 22 when I went to work is Silicon Valley.

While Chinese is my first language, Taiwanese culture is very different from Chinese culture. It is interesting that all the Taiwanese game companies have failed in China and have returned to Taiwan. One clear difference between China and Taiwan is Communism: Taiwan was never a Communist country.

One of the many aspects of Communism was materialism. Creativity is about making something out of nothing—that doesn't fit well with a philosophy that is based on materialism. The Cultural Revolution got rid of the artisan and intellectual classes—the benefits of art and learning were not understood and were not valued, and so they were systematically erased from Chinese society.

The Cultural Revolution also reduced the influence of a lot of old values including Taoism, Confucianism, and the other ancient Chinese philosophies (such as the notion of Yin and Yang, Feng Shui, and Chinese medicine). Some values have gone and others are not as strong as might be expected, although these values are still prevalent in Taiwan, Hong Kong, and Singapore.

Having spent time in Silicon Valley, by 2005 I found myself working in China. It was time to go out on my own again and this was when I formed Radiance. For me, there was only one way to go when developing games: MMOGs (or massive multiplayer online games).

Massive Multiplayer Online Games

At Radiance we develop massive multiplayer online games. These are games, played online (on the internet) where there might be hundreds of players simultaneously. Unlike conventional console games, the game (or the world of the game) continues when a player is not present in the world.

The development of MMOGs requires huge amounts of creativity and understanding:

- First, there is the development of a game itself. Among other things, this needs people to be able to visualize and really "understand" the alternate world that is being created.

- Then there are the technological aspects of games—in addition to the plot lines, the graphics, and the coding (to give three examples) you have to make the thing work online. This again requires huge amounts of creativity and problem solving abilities.

My Introduction to MMOG

I've always been a console guy: X-Box, PlayStation and so on. I love the console business—it's clean and it's what I do the best. In 1999 I played EverQuest (from Sony Online Entertainment) and I knew in my gut that this was going to revolutionize the game industry. This was going to be the next killer app for the internet. I felt this was going to be the future and I soon grasped that console games would be connected online as well. As we now know, this is slowly happening.

To the non-Asian games maker, MMOGs are a niche market. However, online games are the reality in China and have been for the last 8 years. The main reason for this is software piracy: in China and in Asia packaged games do not have a market because anything in a physical form such as a CD or a DVD will be copied. Not might—will be pirated.

While this type of game may appear niche to some people, it is very of the moment and is an area that is undergoing huge growth. For us it was half a conscious decision and half a lucky accident that we entered this market.

The Business Necessity for MMOG

The MMOG business model provides protection against the pirates, but it also provides many other benefits for the producer.

This model generates more revenue per product and there is ongoing subscription revenue rather than a one-off hit that you get from selling a product. So as a service-based product you're getting a residual income. In addition as the publisher you have an ongoing relationship with the consumer which means you can build and foster much stronger customer loyalty.

The other key advantage from this business model is that there are no manufacturing and distribution costs (in the conventional sense): people download the game. There are the infrastructure costs with a lot of people downloading, but the servers are a lot less expensive than the cost of a packaged game where the retailers would also take a large cut.

Perhaps I can best illustrate the economics of the business by talking a bit about the numbers. In the online market we have ARPU: average revenue per user, and ACU: average concurrent users. This is how you gauge the success of an online game. If a game hits 100,000 ACU, then that is a huge success. In China an average person would pay $10 per month, so if a game has an ACU of 100,000 then it will generate an income $12 million per year.

Product or Service

If a game is online then it's not a product, it's a service. It's a lot harder to pirate a service, for instance, you need servers locked away in a data center, firewalls, and guys to maintain the servers. Even if the pirates could steal the software, they can't replicate the kind of service that the game companies can offer to their audience.

For an analogy, it's easy for pirates to copy DVDs, but it's really hard to take over a whole TV network. A TV network is like an online game company and the online game companies have to be constantly coming up with new content to feed their user base like a TV company who can't run out of programs on a Friday night. Because of this business environment, online games have become the only viable business model in China (and Korea and Taiwan).

New Phenomenon

The online game market is creating a whole new phenomenon in China which, as I said, is very much of the moment.

There are urban professionals spending hundreds and thousands of dollars on the games they want. They don't care about the cost because there are no other better forms of entertainment in China. In a lot of Chinese cities there are so few forms of entertainment and people don't have much else to do even though they have money in their pockets. The lack of a developed wide-range consumer market means that people have a limited choice about where to spend their money. Luckily, one choice they have is online games.

Playing games online anonymously with other people has become a huge phenomenon. Young people do it and so do people in their 30s. White collar staff working in an office in Shanghai or Shenzhen will now play online games.

It's now hip to play online games. If you don't play online games or know about the latest online game trends in China, then you have dated yourself and identified yourself as being somewhat out of touch.

For guys in their 30s who aren't married, this has also become a really good way to meet girls. There is no pub/bar and/or nightclub scene in most of China. People are also generally very shy. Online games give people the chance to get to know other people in a virtual world before they get to meet them in real life. This is very attractive to a lot of young people and takes a lot of pressure out of dating.

Why Stay in China

There is one other key advantage to starting our games in China: the Chinese consumer is more resilient. They can deal with faulty products, so this is a perfect place to try things.

We have found ourselves in an interesting position, and even American companies are coming to China to pick products or to license product to take back to the US. On one hand our products are cheaper, and on the other hand our business model and technology are more advanced than the US although our industry has only been around for about eight years. It might have been around for longer in the US, but only for a few games—here it's the whole market. It's a case of five or ten US games versus hundreds of successful games in China.

And that brings us to the ultimate irony—and perhaps a compelling reason why the Chinese games market may grow to have global dominance—although our labor *may* be cheaper, we have more experience than people from other more expensive markets.

Against that background, let me tell you about how I built Radiance.

Radiance: Forming (June 2005 to June 2006)

In June of 2005, I left Shanda and was ready to get Radiance started.

I had an assistant at the time, he is a native Shanghainese, which was important—I am sure we saved about 30% on everything we purchased because he was able to haggle in the local dialect. I never showed my face—it's never a smart thing to show my foreigner's face during a haggle in China as the price will automatically rise (and keep rising).

In retrospect, the first year we were in business was really a baby stepping year. I learned to manage and work with my staff, and we learned to do business as a Chinese company with foreign companies. We learned to set up a Chinese company and started learning the rules of the game in Chinese business world.

Radiance Corporate Structure

When I was starting Radiance, the first thing I did was find a law firm that would help me set up a British Virgin Island company which is the holding company. My assistant then helped me find a local Chinese law firm to set up a WOFE (Wholly-Owned Foreign Enterprise). The WOFE is the main corporate entity through which we conduct business in China.

If you come to China you will hear from a lot of Chinese domestic companies telling you how impossible it is for foreigners to do business in China: they either don't want you to be in China or they will want you to form a joint venture with them under their watch and control. My recommendation is not to do this: it's a lot more fun to navigate your own way in China. It may be harder and it may take longer, but I think it is worth it.

A WOFE has other benefits such as reduced income tax and a rent/equipment purchase subsidy. However most of the countrywide pro-foreign investment policies are being phased-out. If you are a foreign investor looking to get these sorts of benefits today, you will find them in the second tier cities and from the provincial governments.

The reason I set up a BVI (British Virgin Island) holding company was because of the tax treatment, and the Cayman Islands' annual maintenance fee was much higher than the BVI corporate maintenance fee. When companies are ready for an IPO—for example, on NASDAQ—then they change the jurisdiction of the company to the Caymans where companies are more visible from a US regulatory perspective.

Logistics of Setting Up an Office

We had a temporary office in a residential building: the floor was sticky and the hallways were dark. Some of the candidates we interviewed said they need to use the bathroom and never came back.

We stayed in that temporary office for a month, I think... The memory is so traumatic; I sort of block it out. I just remember it being a gross place where I rarely spent anytime. I was very motivated to find a real office space, so I spent most of the time office hunting.

We realized that an office in a residential location wasn't the best way to get things started. A professional looking office gives candidates confidence—they won't think you're pulling some kind of scam—and a clean office is much more conducive to a creative atmosphere.

I got all the co-founders and initial employees together in a local café, and I told them to go off, relax, and come back to the new office in a month. We leased an office in a prime location—this was a purpose-built office building and the floor wasn't sticky!!

We spent some money remodeling the office; a month later everyone came back and started working hard. Having a professional working environment was more important than I had originally expected.

Behaving Like "the Boss"

In China, most employees work in cubicles with short dividers between them. Radiance is the same, and we also have a lot of meeting rooms in the office. Only our finance and human resource people have their own offices due to the confidential nature of the material they handle.

By reputation, and sometimes by practice, staff in the creative industries do not get on well with the "suits". Creative people can resent status-driven decisions at the office: they resent one member of staff having an office while another doesn't. I am very supportive of that position. Status and past achievements can make one lazy, and in our industry, you are only as good as the last product you produced.

As the boss, I didn't want to separate myself from my people. I wanted to work in a cubicle just like my staff so that I could be in the same work environment, and could learn more about them and their needs. I also hoped this would help them to find me more approachable.

However, for my staff this was an alien concept—they could not make that mental leap. My staff would not allow me to sit in a cube: they said "a boss needs to look like a boss".

So I was forced into having a CEO's office. My staff wanted the boss to have a certain level of privilege which would make them proud. If I turned up at the office in sandals and shorts, that would not inspire confidence. This attitude is quite unique to China: I know numerous Silicon Valley executives who have ponytails, wear Hawaiian shirts, shorts, and sandals all year long. For me, the China experience is very East Coast—old school and old values

For my office, I choose Chinese Qin dynasty reproduction antique furniture: I designed it myself and a factory built everything for my office for 5,000 RMB. This furniture would easily cost US $5,000 in the United States. If I had wanted Western office furniture—which would have been much less interesting than what I have—then I would have had to pay a lot more than I would in the United States. This was a good lesson for me, when in Rome...

5,000 RMB Chinese furniture would cost $5,000 in the US but $2,000 of Western furniture would cost me $5,000 in China.

Now I always get praised when people who come into my office. It is a very cool office!! Sometimes you need to be a little bit more flexible in your expectations in order to be pleasantly surprised by what you get.

Stock Options and Other Ways of Paying People

One of the challenges we had in the early days—and we still have this issue today to a certain degree—is that Chinese employees do not understand the value of stock options.

They want cash.

This situation does not help entrepreneurs starting up new businesses and there is really no way around it. You need to do a lot of education and the effect will still be very limited. Sometimes, you need to consider not hiring an employee who doesn't care about stock options.

I believe the attraction of stock options is not as big as we would like it to be because China has only seen how capitalism works in the past 15-20 years. The people have not seen enough option holders becoming rich from stock options to want it for themselves. Even when the public is aware of certain celebrity executives who got rich from IPOs, they do not understand the mechanism of how it happens.

When I come to pay people—and when I want to give them a real incentive to deliver and deliver in a way that help the business succeed—there are two deeply ingrained challenges in China:

- Local employees come with their own perceptions and expectations. There are things they understand and there are things they don't want to understand. Stock options are one thing they don't want to understand. Instead, they want cash.

- The labor laws in China are different to those in many other countries. In China you sign people on for at least a year. If I let somebody go—for whatever reason—then I still have to compensate the individual, even if the employee is unethical or simply not performing well. Even after the end of the year's contract, if the contract is not renewed, we still have to pay the (former) employee a severance payment calculated as a month's salary for each year of the contract.

In Radiance we do have performance-based bonuses, but in a socialist-based state such as China, people have a high entitlement-mentality which means that they take the bonuses for granted. They will forget that these are performance-based. To keep overheads down it is common to keep base salary as low as possible and give more performance-based pay. But we then found that when we tried to recruit people we had less bargaining power since people did not perceive any value in the fluctuating pay on offer, especially as the job market is so highly competitive.

In any event, we already have to pay one or two months' salary as a year-end bonus for Chinese New Year. This means that typically we are paying 13-14 months' salary a year and then we have milestone-based bonuses on top of that.

As an entrepreneur in the US I used to worry about the Christmas bonuses—in China, it's the year end bonuses.

Because people are so insistent in their expectations for base pay, we're looking at other options. So for instance, instead of simply meeting people's expectations we might pay halfway between what we want to pay and what they want to be paid. Then we will pay an additional bonus to take them to the level that they want—this bonus will only be paid if they remain employed with us for 12 months. This means people will get what they want but forfeit the additional payment if they leave earlier than expected.

Patience

In the early days of Radiance, I tended to shake my head a lot when I saw things that were out of order, whether in my business or elsewhere. I have observed the same behaviors with other ex-pats—in fact, I believe when a group of ex-pat CEOs get together, the common topic of conversation is to complain about their Chinese employees.

I was one of them. The attitude I had back then, was apathetic: I either accepted the situation as it was, or I would complain, and complaining did not improve my situation.

I don't know about other people's experiences, but it did not work when I told an employee "I am sure I told you not to do it this way, why did you do it that way?" When I treated my employees as if they are stupid, they become stupid.

When I realized my old behaviors weren't helping my business I became more empathetic and nurturing. Most importantly, now I show people how to do what I want them to do. In China, what worked (and still works) the best for me was when I rolled up my sleeves, and showed how I would do something.

For instance, what I still do with my businesses development staff is blind copy them when I send an email to clients. In this way I help to teach them how to write professional looking business emails in English. Sometimes I put the clients on the speaker phone and I show my staff how I negotiate.

The teaching never stops: I believe when I don't have to teach anymore, that is the time I should go away to retire or do something else.

Chasing Dream Projects

Certain projects we thought would happen never did.

We worked with a Korean company NC Soft and Disney Internet Group for six months but neither became a real project. We kept making demos for them, but for political reasons or business reasons that we did not understand, the project never happened.

We over-extended ourselves and we bent over backwards to try to please our prospective clients. Then when we looked at our investment in these projects which hadn't generated a cent of income but which had cost us a lot, we decided that this behavior wasn't smart. We literally wasted nine months and had no revenue because of this approach.

Many startup CEOs think this is a necessary evil because they are in a chicken and egg situation. I felt that way too: I understood we had to produce an egg somehow, but that wasn't the end of the story. Once we had the egg, the important thing was to make sure the egg was incubated and then hatched a healthy chick.

However, many things can go wrong before you get a healthy chick and these problems can arise in many places.

We worked for nine months and had nothing to show. If we had spent that time trying to make our own game, we would have finished half of it and it would then have only taken another nine months to have our first product. If we had followed this route, we would have launched our first product in December 2006.

But that didn't happen.

Instead, what happened was that we had to start over and we didn't ship our first game until July of 2008: our first hatched chick. This might sound bad, but it isn't. We learned our lessons and we moved on. If we had learned the wrong lessons, we would still be stuck in that deadlock cycle.

After all our wasted time, when we finally got our first business contract, the Chinese client decided not to pay us on time.

We became a little bit more cynical, a bit more critical about our prospects, and learned from this. We are still happy to do small amounts of demonstration work, but now we want to be compensated for the trial work we do. If a prospect doesn't agree that we should be paid for the trial work, then we will move on. We will not over-extend ourselves, especially when a prospect has not demonstrated their commitment to us and the project by laying down money.

Sometimes by taking this approach we gain respect from our customer.

We made these mistakes in the forming stage and we have not repeated them.

Operating in Stealth Mode

When we first set up Radiance we operated in stealth mode for about six months. During this time we did not want any attention from anyone—in particular former employers. We wanted to be left alone so we could build the company.

We tried to stay stealthy for as long as possible because attention in China can lead to a lot of trouble.

For the first six months no one knew where the company was located, what we were working on, or where I lived. Maybe I was being paranoid, but it was better to be safe than sorry: when we were young and fragile, people could do us real damage and shake the confidence of our employees by spreading rumors.

Being stealthy meant that we couldn't do any PR activities so we had to focus on the things we should be focusing on: building the company and building great products. This gave much better results than would have been achieved by doing PR for a company that was too young and had no product. Lack of outward activities forced us to do inner works.

In China you never gain any respect by telling people that you are good. The Confucian and Taoist influences teach that modesty is a virtue, and anyone in China who ignores this is regarded as a poor business leader or part of a poor company. The saying "any PR is good PR", does not work in China.

Status and reputation come in China because you deserve status or reputation, not because you say you do. You need the underlying business to back up any status or reputation, and being humble is part of having a good reputation. The emphasis on PR will backfire if you don't focus on the products which will give you a good reputation.

Even today, humility can be good for us. We have just launched a new game and nobody knows we are the company behind the game, and I don't want them to know, because it is not necessary to know who made the game to decide whether you like it or not. If people like the game, then they will try to find out who produced it and when they find we built the game and they liked it, then hopefully they will respect us even more for keeping a low profile.

Shameless self-promotion is a real shame in China.

Radiance: Storming (July 2006 to June 2007)

A lot of the work in setting up the company—such as finding office space and hiring staff—has nothing to do with doing business. Sure, you can't run a business without staff and with the number of people we had, we needed an office, but our business is making games, not setting up an office!!

After we had finished forming the company—and getting all of the structure in place so that we could do business—we could focus on storming: bringing people together to create products which could be delivered to clients in exchange for money.

During the second year of Radiance, we fell over a lot. As Murphy's law states: anything that can go wrong, will go wrong. We made all the mistakes there were to make. This was the year of losing staff, a failed project, delayed productions, a customer who did not pay, and more... However, we learned from the mistakes and moved on to flourish.

Bilingual Staff and Cultural References

Six months after we moved into our wonderful office on a business street in a professional office building (without sticky floors) next to a six star hotel (the St Regis, where Putin stayed during his visit to Shanghai), the Shanghai government decided to shut down the nearest subway station. This made our location isolated and very difficult to reach.

At the same time, a local art university, the Shanghai Theatre Academy, granted me an honorary professor title and invited us to move our office to the university campus. The rent was half the market rate, and taking all matters into consideration, we made the move. In making our move, we kept all our employees with one exception: my assistant. Her commute would go from 30 minutes to an hour each way.

As a foreigner, if you are working in China and you do not have a bilingual assistant, then you are in trouble. You cannot communicate with people, you don't know how to organize meetings and get things done. You are isolated in China. Ideally, if you are not a native-English speaker, then your assistant's spoken languages should also include English (since that is very often the lingua franca of business).

Although I speak Chinese, I need a bilingual assistant because we have many more foreign customers than domestic customers. Also, half my business contacts within China are English speakers and my assistant has to be able to call them to schedule meetings.

Finding a good English-speaking assistant really is a challenge in China: you usually have to hire and then work with an assistant before you know that you've found a good one. And when you find a good assistant, they will then quit when they find a better offer as there is such a huge demand for people with these skills. It took me another two or three months before I found my current assistant.

Our lack of language skill within the company was again highlighted in January 2007, when we signed a contract with Google headquarters to do a lot of art work for their virtual community project. As well as language, we had other cultural issues. One of the characters we built is an African American called Ty (code name: Afro dude). Ty has a huge fro, walks with a jive, and has a hair comb in his fro. None of my Chinese staff get it, so they could not produce what Google wanted. In the end, Google had to video one of their employees doing the jive walk.

This isn't a linguistic issue, it's cultural. Chinese society was very closed for many years and so it is quite understandable that the Chinese have no reference points for the African American caricature. Perhaps if they had been exposed to Shaft (and the other blaxploitation movies), Bill Cosby, the Harlem Globetrotters, or the Jackson 5 (to give a few international reference points) things may have been different. Equally, there are many other cultural references (such as Disney) that are known and accepted in the West, but unheard of by many Chinese.

In all honesty, we did the Google project well; the only problem was our staff's English skills which weren't good enough to allow them to freely communicate well with Google US employees. We tried many things, but in the end we had to hire an American to do the job well. On demanding projects, bilingual doesn't cut it: you need native speakers on that those projects.

Employee Turnover

During this period we suddenly lost eight employees: all of them were important, one of them was a co-founder. A lot of people want go out on their own: there are lots and lots of startups in China and the cost of entry into business is very low. Many employers lose employees and see vital trade secrets—such as their customer list or computer source code—walk out the door. This is very common, but fortunately was not the case for us.

A real challenge when trying to keep staff in China is that people rarely speak up about the issues that they face. They will voice that they need a pay rise, but that is about it: they will never come and tell you what's on their mind.

Even when they leave, they make up stories such as someone in their family is sick and they have to go back, or in some cases, they claim that they are going back to school. This is especially the case when the fact is they can't handle the work: they just make something up and quit rather than lose face or risk a confrontation. This means that it is difficult to learn why people are leaving.

Many people know that the influence of Confucius resonates through Asia. However, few people know what Confucius stood for, nor the implications of his influence on today's society in China.

The core thinking of Confucianism is that the society has to have a certain order:

- the father has to act like a father and a son has to act like a son

- the emperor has the unconditional respect from those who serve him

- the elders are owed respect, and

- everyone has their place in society, this historically included women staying at home, raising children and serving their husbands.

This philosophy is deeply ingrained in the Chinese psyche. Talking back to the boss is unconscionable and expressing disagreement is also very difficult for them. For these reasons, I received no signals from the people who wanted to leave the company, and I was not given an opportunity to address any of their concerns.

Those two months were like a roller coaster ride: we all went through the ups and downs. After we re-staffed all of the positions, we all looked back with disbelief—not only did we replace the positions but we got cheaper and even more qualified people who were enthusiastic to perform!

Pride in Work

In my personal experience, less than 10% of employees in China take ownership and pride in their work. While this is quite unsettling, I find personal coaching irreplaceable and the results are usually stunningly great.

There is a saying in China: "the birds that fly out of the forest will be shot down". Most Chinese understand the value in laying low and not attracting attention: they believe that more bad than good will come if they draw attention to themselves. The pressure from Chinese society to conform usually outweighs the desire for self-expression.

During the Cultural Revolution the rich and the powerful were thrown into labor camps and stripped of their wealth.

This was a very practical demonstration of why people should keep their head down and not be ambitious.

To recondition this state of mind, I have had to make sure I always reward the problem spotter. But I have to be very careful about opening the flood gates: it is very possible to open a can of worms, and start employees finger pointing and bickering. My key focus has been to direct energy to constructive problem solving—venting is fine—but what is more valuable to the business is to be a problem solver.

Growing up in Taiwan, I was often labeled as a troublemaker. When I went to Silicon Valley, sometimes I was labeled a loose cannon (but in a good way), so I can relate to the other like-minded individuals who have grown up in a highly suppressed environment. I have learned to be empathetic and help them direct their "loose cannon" energy in a positive direction so that they became heroes in the company. This may not be the best way to manage a company, but given the circumstances, I have to give other employees a few role models to look up to.

What I found helpful is to teach honor, pride, and courage. Of course when all fails, I resort to guilt-tripping. A sense of guilt is so deeply rooted in our psyche and it works in most cultures. I hate doing it because empowering people with shame is such a negative experience, and it usually does not last very long. But when I realize I can't even guilt-trip an employee, then it's time to get hiring.

The First Income-Generating Project

We were so disappointed with the way we initially did business. We wanted a customer to pay for the work we did and so we found a local Chinese company that would engage us to develop a new game which they would then publish. As part of the deal, we would keep the intellectual property rights.

This sounded like a great deal. We didn't want to get into the publishing business and the Chinese company didn't want to get into game development business... We would get to do what we love to do and get paid for it!

We received the first payment after we signed the agreement and that was the only payment that was ever on time.

The terms of the contract placed no requirements on us. It soon became clear that this was because they did not know what they wanted. So we kept trying different ideas for them and even after they accepted our proposed milestones, getting paid was another story.

Many industries in China are young and inexperienced, they don't know what they want and they don't know how to specify their requirements. Essentially, people don't know what they don't know.

This is why it is easier for companies to take a finished product and decide it is exactly what they want. This situation is one of the roots of the lack of innovation in China which leads to a duplication culture with no development. Worse still, everyone is afraid of trying and failing.

To get paid my financial manager used to go to the client's office and sit in the front lobby waiting for their finance people. There was always a line of people waiting to be paid: it wasn't that they didn't have any money, it was just poor business practices.

When it came to payment collection, they didn't reply to emails, and didn't answer phone calls, so I ended up paying most of my employees out of my own pocket. Our monthly burn rate for 30 game developers was US$30,000: that was our cost, and for 17 months of work we only received four months payment totaling $120,000.

We terminated the contract in February of 2008 and then retained a law firm to send contract termination notices. Our former client did not even respond to these.

It is a common situation to have difficulty getting paid by a Chinese company, so when one pays on time they get a lot more businesses. In my view, trust is one of the challenges that is holding back the growth of many industries in China.

I have learned from this heartbreaking and financially painful experience. Payment collection is something to be taken very seriously and now I always build-in late payment penalties for all of our agreements. More significantly, I only enter a business arrangement where we have leverage, and I'm not afraid to send lawyers in to make the other party's lives miserable: it's only fair.

When looking for leverage, I look for a way to keep some control after the signing of agreements and after we deliver the product. One example of this would be to ensure that the product needs ongoing support or it will stop functioning. This is a defensive way of thinking but most Chinese companies think that way too. They always try to think of ways not to get stuffed. The win/win scenario is not often seen in my line of business, nor in China.

As for suing your customer or not, that used to be a real tough choice for me, but after seeing my life savings diminish because of my indecision, it is no longer such a difficult issue for me anymore. I have no aspiration to play Hamlet in a Shakespearean tragedy: now I either do the work and get paid, or I just walk away.

Radiance Enters Expansion Mode

I had a taste of what not getting paid would do to us, so I wanted to work with more foreign companies. I saw having more export business as a hedge against our domestic business.

We had our existing project, and then in January of 2007 we took on the Google online community project, and we also signed an agreement with the biggest online game company in Vietnam. In February of 2007, we got another project from a German firm to build an online game. All of a sudden, we had four teams working on four different projects.

In my early career, I had some experience of having to staff up quickly to get a product completed. In the US, getting products done on time is a matter of life and death, because half of the sales in a year happen during the Christmas seasons.

From those experiences, I learned to work well with human resource departments, and learned to make them my best friends. In my mind, human resources is one of the most important functions in a software/creative company. However, I hadn't realized what value the human resource people could bring to the business in China.

Foreigners running businesses in China need to be aware that you can't just fire someone: China is a socialist state and the labor laws are very one-sided to protect the workers. Even with cause, you will have to make severance payments. I have always found it critical to have human resource professionals in my company to make sure everything is within the rules. As well as helping with the hiring and firing, human resources can provide a place for people to vent and can proactively seek out discontent before it becomes an issue.

The German Project

A successful German game publisher decided to outsource the online version their famous game to China. They did three or four months of due diligence on Korean companies, many Chinese companies, and one company in Romania. Chinese and Korean companies are very good at making online games where very few Western companies have experience with this approach. By contrast, the US companies tend to over-spend on, and over-engineer their online products.

Radiance was chosen for the project mainly because we proved that we could accomplish the work and we were the most cost-effective. As they wanted to get their product into the Chinese market (the biggest online game market in the world) we had another advantage.

China is a great place to make games because its market is big enough, there are a lot of enthusiastic players in the population, and added to which making games is a hip and respectable profession. India has similar cost structure to China, but the game industry is non-existent and even when the Indian programmers can make games, their game artists do not produce the style of work that the rest of the world wants. However, this is changing as some of the Hollywood animation movies are getting made in India now. That being said, I still believe the gaming market needs to exist in India before India can be a place for game production.

For this project, the German firm hired a temporary technical director (an American) to come to our office for one week. He went over every line of our source code and in the end we got his stamp of approval.

During the production, the German customer was demanding: they checked our source code all the time so we really felt like we were constantly being micromanaged. We literally had someone looking over our shoulder every step of the way.

Towards the end of this project we were spread too thinly (partly because of this approach) and eventually we hired senior engineer to join the project, but it was too late. I had long talks with the CEO of the firm and tried to explain to him that he couldn't expect to have Western standards of delivery (in terms of quality and timing) while only paying a

Chinese price. I asked him to have a little more patience, but he didn't have any.

If we had more time, we could have corrected the quality. I was willing to fix the quality on my dime, but we were not given that chance.

The issue was that the Germans thought it was easy and other studios could do it too. The reality was the cheaper studios couldn't do what we did and the studio that could deliver would cost a lot more than the client was willing to pay. The German firm's original assessments were correct—Radiance was the best bang for the buck—but they wanted their level of quality without having to wait.

The Chinese people focus on results, as long as the results are good, they don't care how the work gets done. By contrast, the Germans wanted this project done in a certain way and this level of scrutiny was not the case for the first 80% of the project with the original (temporary) technical director. Towards the end of the project they hired a new technical director who used an absolute scale to measure our software engineers. On his scale, we didn't measure up.

The Chinese way certainly works, sometimes the process is ugly, but the process will eventually get the products out the door. However, perhaps it takes a little more time.

We ended up terminating the project. After this the client looked for other studios to do the work but they couldn't find any company that was willing to work with them on their pay scale, and eventually they folded the business.

This experience taught me that I can have ultimate patience with my people and my business partners, but I can't ask the others to have the same patience with us. What could have been a win/win situation turned into a lose/lose situation because our business partner did not have the patience to work out the kinks with us.

I also learned that not every company can work with Chinese companies. The "I want it now!" attitude doesn't work very well between Chinese companies and foreign companies.

Radiance: Norming (July 2007 to June 2008)

Once we had experienced the storming stage, we continued to build the business by moving on to the norming stage where we took on more projects and put a lot of processes in place. It was at this point that we started to really understand our weaknesses and the projects that would not suit our business.

Real change takes time in China, so we gradually put the processes in place. We avoided projects that would require micromanagement and large amounts of overseas communications. Instead of fixing our weaknesses, we avoided exposing or amplifying them.

We were more skeptical and careful about new customers, partners, and even employees. We had a well-oiled game-making machine, formal process for reviewing agreements, a standard format for non-disclosure agreements, employment contracts, and performance evaluation on semi-annual basis. With the two games that were near completion, we started thinking how we could maximize our value.

Fierce Conversations with Venture Capitalists

In February of 2007, I started talking with venture capitalists. I was looking for investors in Radiance to make sure we could complete all our products. I ran into two kinds of venture capitalists.

The first kind only wanted to invest in outsourcing studios, because they could understand the manufacturing in China concept, but they didn't understand the video game industry (and didn't have the patience to understand). What I could not convince them was that there is a very low entry barrier in that business, and at the end of day, those sorts of businesses will have to raise their prices to pay for increasing salaries in a competitive market with the effect that margins will be slashed.

Maybe trading cheap labor for revenue can work for a mom-and-pop shop operation, but I really couldn't see any IPO or M&A potential. That was 16 months ago, now most of the VCs see things happen the way I saw them and almost none of the art outsourcing studios in China are breaking even.

The second kind of VC saw the success of many Chinese online game companies. These companies had gone public on NASDAQ, NYSE, and the Hong Kong Exchange. All of them were online game operators (publishers of online content, which are called the operators because they need to provide customer support, online and offline, for a long time after launch). Since the online game industry is a new industry outside China, very few VCs have enough knowledge to make educated assessments of these businesses.

Of all of the VCs I talked to, I was most impressed by Softbank. They are very knowledgeable and they are backed by one of the most successful businesses in Japan. After two or three months of casually talking with them, one day I met up with one of their partners for lunch.

At the time, one of our competitors who started his company six months after I started Radiance raised $8 million dollars based on a $20 million valuation. He had one game in production and a business plan.

I knew that my experience *and* credentials (in terms of name recognition and brand value) were on a higher level than the founder of our competitor and was so frustrated that I got mad and vented at Softbank over lunch. I was also frustrated that my competitor would now get to publish his own games, but knew that the cost of promoting the games was prohibitive at that stage of our business.

The Softbank guy's response was interesting. He suggested a new business model where studios like mine work with internet portals—they promote the games to their members and we then share revenue with them. This would mean that I would not have to spend any money on promotion.

He then agreed to introduce me to one of his contact (which he duly did). I went to Beijing and met with the CEO of that company, we hit it off, and he liked our products. We knew we could do business together.

When I came back, Softbank signed outline terms with us and began four months of due diligence, finally closing our first round of funding with a financial institution.

I was impressed—and it has fostered great trust and respect—that Softbank waited until after we had agreed the business (in other words, after we were in a stronger negotiating position) before they negotiated the investment with us.

Monte's Paradox

Over the years of working in a creative industry I have learned that the freedom to be creative is a perk for creative workers. When you take that freedom away, the work is no more than a job.

Many art outsourcing studios in China have lost many employees over the years. We keep hearing that these people want to work on an original game, not just take orders from someone and do as they are told. With that mind, I often have to bite my tongue in meetings or when my employees are showing me a demo.

My comments carry a lot more weight than I am willing to accept: when I say "good", that may be interpreted as "great" or "that's done, don't spend any more work on it". If I give any negative feedback, it could trigger all kinds of drama and

I will get deafened with excuses like they are short-handed or not enough time was allowed for them to do good work. Not unsurprisingly, people get defensive.

This means that I have found myself in dilemma in that I am the most experienced game developer in the building—and I am the founder of the business—but I can't give any input.

I don't want my developers to lose their passion and I also don't want them to go in the wrong direction. I may know the shortcuts and I know many of the pitfalls for the unwary (since I made the same mistakes in the past) but I can't tell people or I will lose them.

One thing I got over very quickly was that I cannot let my ego get in the way. I may be a very seasoned game developer, but I have not done any coding for over 10 years, and back when I did code, I never worked on any online games. I have to stay humble and only offer my opinion when I am asked or when my colleagues are in trouble.

My creative energy has to find its outlets or there is a chance I will get myself into trouble at work, so I have learned to compose music. Some of the music may get incorporated into the games or it may not, but at least it keeps me busy with my private time.

I also spend my time looking forward and developing strategies for our next projects. I get to brainstorm with my peers in the industry (some are CEOs and some are the best game makers in the world). The key is for me to reconcile my needs to create and being a good business leader for my company. I do this by channeling my energy to benefit my business and not to satisfy my ego.

It's All Good

It is a Chinese custom at the end of each lunar year that the company treats the entire workforce to a banquet. The 2007 year end banquet was the biggest ever: beer and foul-tasting

50% alcohol rice liquor called baijiu were in order. Singing, dancing, crying, and puking were part of the ritual: it is the only day of the entire year that you see the other staff as people who have the full spectrum of emotions.

We had a senior programmer who was going back to home to help his uncle start up a new business: after the year end dinner, he decided to stay. One of our board members from Softbank puked with us. I walked home that night in the snow, telling myself: "it is all good".

Radiance: Performing

Recently we have moved into the performing stage. I have noticed that we are doing a lot less dreaming and a lot more doing—solidifying energy into matter, turning hard work into revenue.

In the creative industries, it is crucial to make a separation between being creative and execution. While I am being creative—and ultimately, I got into the business to be creative—I am not delivering product. Therefore at a certain point, it is crucial that as CEO I ensure we move from the "art" of the product to the "craft": in other words, to finishing the product and getting it out the door.

One challenge with any project is that the creative input happens at the start when the project is defined. That phase is short and once it is done, the rest of the work is executing that vision. There may be a need for some creative problem solving, but it is mostly about focusing on the tasks that need to be achieved.

The other irony of our business is that ideas are cheap. Any idea *could* work. It takes so much money and hard work to turn an idea into a real product. Any idea could become a game—the question is whether the idea can be executed and whether the product could then be commercially successful. The idea takes a second... the execution is much harder.

The Necessity to Finish

The message from our venture capital investor was clear: we needed to become an operator to make the business more valuable. Also with the VC cash injection, the realization came that I no longer had any more cash to put into the company: when the money runs out, that's that. End of game, quite literally. This means that I have had to direct my energy and resources and make sure they are used in areas that will create the most value for the company.

The most valuable thing for the company at the time we got the investment were the two projects we had in production. We utilized that money and focused on getting the projects done. This has meant that in the last year I've forced myself to behave like a horse with blinders: all I can see is what's ahead of me and what I need to do to reach that goal. I make sure I stay focused and won't let myself get distracted.

People ask me what my next project will be and I tell them I don't want to think about it. Now, of course, I cannot NOT think about my next project—I'm a creative guy and our long-term business depends on developing new projects—however, if we can't deliver our current projects, then there will be no long term business and there will be no next project. So I don't think about new projects more than I need to, and I certainly don't talk about possible, potential, new long-term projects.

I have to make the current dream come true, for me and the company. Once I have done that, then I can dream the next dream.

The Process of Finishing Game Production

Creating products is like the process of carrying a baby, and shipping products is like giving birth, with a lot of pain, a lot of tears, and ultimately, joy. When the time comes, the product needs to leave the building, one way or another.

Because of time and cost constraints, all commercial product developments have deadlines. Towards the end of the production cycle, the producer or project manager has to perform "triage" to prioritize the features and determine which features to keep and which features to cut. Going back to the metaphor of giving birth to a baby, deciding which limb(s) to cut off is extremely difficult especially at its birth.

Most of the online games in China will be played by hundreds of thousands of players, if not millions. This means developers and managers get cold feet and start back-peddling as the release date approaches. We have a QA (quality assurance) department to ensure the product measures up in terms of quality and performance. An additional benefit of the QA department is that if they bless a product, not only does the production team feel relieved, but the company also feels more confident about releasing the game into the market.

The problem with most game developers is a lack of objectivity. Once objectivity has gone you can't tell whether you're working on a piece of junk or the best game ever. Part of the function of the QA department is to keep the objectivity. They rate the quality and the progress of the project. Only by having a group of people who are separate from the project can we maintain that objectivity.

In the final stage of shipping products, I need producers who will behave like dictators and listen to no excuses: people who take names and yell at me for talking to their staff. I call this type of person a "missionary man": through my entire 22 year career I was only managed by one producer who was like this. He was an American from Oklahoma. By contrast, almost every Japanese producer I have met is a missionary.

In China, people cherish "harmony" at the expense of product quality, employees' growth, and the company's bottom line. My managers are uncomfortable telling their subordinates that they have made mistakes and that they need to adjust their behavior. It is even difficult for them to do one-on-one meetings—those are too intimate for most managers. The solution is a massive amount of training and role playing to show them how to do it.

Learning to Criticize

The criticisms from me that people are most willing to listen to are those relating to the company bottom line. So if I can make a case where a certain action will have a positive effect on the bottom line, or maybe that inactivity in a certain area will have negative consequences, my argument will be much more convincing. However, I have to be very sure of my ground here: I cannot misuse statistics. But if I am honest and upfront, and can make a link, then I will influence.

For instance, at the moment we are working on the English localization of a game. I was asked whether this could be postponed. I was happy for there to be a delay, provided they could show me where I could find the $300,000 I am expecting when the English version is made available. My point was understood and proper follow up actions were taken by the developers.

Single Issue Focus

On the creative side, I have learned to pick my battles. I don't want our employees to feel that I have muscled in and insisted that things are done my way. If the only thing the boss can say is negative, then people are going to become numb and stop listening. At that point it doesn't matter how good or how valid my point is: my comment will change nothing.

My main way to keep focus is by setting a single objective.

If I have a team and their ability would be rated at five, but I need them to be at seven, then there is nothing I can do to *make* them improve. The only way is to address one feature at a time and I do this by initially rallying the senior staff in the company. I have to educate them and brainwash them—I will stress on one subject, and only one subject. At any given moment there will always be one—and only one—hot subject.

Slowly, as each issue is adopted and integrated into everyday behavior, the performance of the teams will improve such that they go from a five, to a six, to a seven. When that subject is fully addressed, I will move on to the next subject.

I'm never going to be happy with the level of creativity in the company, but I have to prioritize. I also have to consider that certain features will take a lot more money and time to implement, so from a practical perspective, we can't do everything. Sometimes knowing that there are budget or practical constraints lowers people's enthusiasm for a project.

In addition, focusing on a single issue improves efficiency. If you think about a computer that is multi-tasking, it will devote a certain amount of processing power to each task and will then devote additional power to balancing the power requirements of those separate tasks. The processor power devoted to task management is not being used to achieve any of the tasks, so it is effectively wasted power. Indeed, a computer can devote more power to multi-tasking than it can to actually doing the task.

I don't want people to spend energy deciding which tasks to do and in what order. I want them to understand their priority and deliver. That is a far more efficient way to do business.

As a result—although we work in a creative industry—we can value discipline more. Without discipline, the ideas never become reality. We spend a lot of time enforcing discipline, for instance, employees come in and punch the time clock. If they're late, we dock their pay. It might be brutal, but it is acceptable in China and it helps enforce discipline. There needs to be a framework—you need rules for a game so everyone can enjoy it and we need rules for work so everyone understands where they stand.

Once people get used to our way of working, then they find that they actually have more creative freedom. Instead of channeling freedom into their environment, they channel their energies into creating games. They start to appreciate the freedom they are given.

Lessons Learned

- Look and behave like the boss. Your staff will respect you more for it and you are showing them respect too—to be the boss and not take your position seriously is to show great disrespect to your staff. This is true in China, even in an industry where you are trying to foster a collegiate approach. Behaving like a class clown may be a cool thing to do with your friends, but it is not suitable to do so with your Chinese employees and customers. If you are a goofy type, I recommend you to find outlets in other venues—don't goof while running a Chinese a company.

- It takes time for certain ideas to sink in with your Chinese customers or employees. Prepare them with background information and then give them time to consider the new ideas.

- For some Chinese people in some areas—especially when it comes to management techniques—you have to show them how to do it. Role-play with them or they just won't get how to do it.

- When it comes to creative activities, try to suggest new ideas and do not dictate. Chinese employees take what their CEO says very seriously—your passing comments can cause major anxiety. You also need to consider your "orders" as being the extreme option: don't use it for the small things.

- Hire Chinese people to manage Chinese people. This philosophy came from a Chinese saying "use the foreigners to control the foreigners". Learn from this ancient lesson.

- Get into the regular groove of having weekly meetings, weekly reports, and one-on-one meetings. Chinese employees find comfort in these ritualistic business activities. Use these communication tools to establish checks and balances.

- Be very careful in balancing the forces of ego at the finishing stage of product development. Developers can easily adopt a perfectionist attitude, thinking the product isn't good enough for shipping—this is sometimes caused by fear of inadequacy. The marketing and sales types tend to get overly excited and want to ship the products prematurely—CEOs are usually in this camp. The best way is to find an unbiased third-party to help gauge whether the product is ready for launch.

- Don't flog a dead horse. Certain employees are never going to be your shining stars, so make sure you don't have unrealistic expectations when you hire them, and ensure their salaries are not inflated due to your unreasonable expectations of their performance. A big percentage of employees are going to be the execution types, not the creative types.

- In creative industries, discipline is the biggest challenge. We dock employees' pay for showing to work late, and make sure they don't spend too much time surfing internet, chatting on instant messengers, or playing games... unless they're work-related.

- Have room for mistakes. Don't count on everything going as planned because it won't, especially in a creative industry, especially in China.

- Never say to creative people that things are not the way they were where you came from—try to be more constructive when you are not happy with the status quo. Foreigners have the reputation of being snobby because they look down on cultures that are different. Creative people will not respond well to this.

- Sometimes you need to be a little bit more flexible in your expectations and it can work out a lot better.

Chapter 7

Chinese Style Risk Management: the Need to Diversify

Scott Barrack came to China on a whim having seen a program on CNN. He had been due to go to Germany, but decided to go to China instead, figuring that if nothing else, he would have a great adventure.

He headed for the wild, wild East, not really knowing if Beijing was going to have dirt roads with chickens running around, or whether he would be in the world's most modern city. Like many people, Scott had an idea about the Ming Dynasty and Tiananmen Square, but when his grandmother asked whether there was electricity, he wasn't sure.

All Scott knew was there was a lot of energy being directed to look at China by big American corporations. He didn't know what to expect, but came with an open mind and with a desire to experience everything he could.

In 2000 he started SPACE, a real estate agency, his first venture in China. From this he then started investing in properties—initially investing to quickly sell on, but later developing. The development side of the business grew into a separate business: SPACE Development. The company now develops high end properties: luxury residential properties, serviced apartments, hotels, office complexes, and industrial buildings.

Building on the development side of the business, the natural next move was to create InnShanghai, a group of small-scale serviced apartments. This was to be a stepping stone to the diversification into the URBN Hotel—Shanghai's first boutique hotel (which is also China's first carbon neutral hotel brand).

In this chapter Scott talks about how he grew his business and how he constantly challenges himself to diversify and stay ahead. For Scott, diversification has been both a growth and a risk management strategy.

In retrospect, I made one of my most significant mistakes quite early on. However, this taught me a lasting lesson. I didn't move on from my first business in China (SPACE) quickly enough. Perhaps I had too much emotionally invested, or maybe I was simply naïve and didn't recognize the signs. The end result was that I spent too much time focusing on a business that was no longer strong enough to generate sufficient returns for the time I was investing.

Diversification is not an option in China: it's a necessity because of the legal environment and because of the business environment. Things move so quickly that people have many different businesses to keep flexibility. As a result, often Chinese people will run mini-conglomerates that are highly diversified and where each part may not necessarily have much in common with the other parts.

Everything changes so quickly and what is hot today is cold tomorrow. So diversification is necessary to ensure your whole business isn't wiped out by:

■ A change in the law or the businesses license could mean that your business has become illegal, highly taxed, or restricted to a small group of people. If you've only got one business, then you're out of business if this happens.

■ Your business becoming unprofitable, for instance, in the real estate agency area there was a huge influx of competition which simply didn't exist when I set up. At the same time costs had risen: this has made some aspects of my business unprofitable overnight.

■ Your business getting copied. Again, taking my example, my real estate agency had a business model that could be replicated with little expense and only a little knowledge. This has made the business incredibly vulnerable.

In the case of SPACE, after the business had been running for about two years, the market changed, and changed both dramatically and quickly which meant that we were forever playing catch-up. In retrospect, the sensible move would have been to sell SPACE after the first two years. I have now done what I should have done years ago and have got out of that business.

Getting Started in China

I started my first proper company when I was 25, having been in China for a while. I had gone to school to learn Chinese and then after a short period working in business development, I got into real estate.

I joined forces with a buddy of mine and we started the company that was to become SPACE. After about two years

I bought my partner out and I am still the sole-owner of that brand.

SPACE was the first real estate agency in Shanghai to specialize in properties that would appeal to Western tenants with larger rental budgets. Most property in Shanghai is either very new and very poorly maintained, or very old. There was a tremendous amount of older turn of the century, 1920s/1930s, and art deco properties (often referred to as French Concession) all over the city and there wasn't anybody renting out these places yet. This was the property that interested us and our client base.

We started with a computer and a free office, and not enough money to buy an air conditioning unit. So when the temperature got up around 100° Fahrenheit I took my shirt off to work and dripped on the table. We had very little money and didn't know how long it would last, so we spent as little as possible. Much of the time we asked for favors and got stuff on the cheap: we got a friend of ours to set up our first web site for $150. With our name cards printed and some stationery, we were ready to go.

There's no information (about anything) that is made available to the public in China, added to which the systems are poor (there are no computers) and so reliable records are hard to find. In 2000 it was worse. Our solution was to get on our bicycles and go around different areas of the city to find little lane ways.

Shanghai is split into blocks: historically houses also had small streets in-between houses and even smaller lanes in between these. In these lane ways you will find rows of town houses, old apartments, and small villa complexes. These buildings are old, and because virtually no housing was constructed for about a generation before China started opening up to the outside world, these houses are densely inhabited by the local Chinese population.

We would go out with packets of cigarettes and give them to the locals and the security guards, and ask if anyone had a property that they wanted to sell or rent. We were the only laowai (foreigners, or more literally, old outsiders) doing real estate who spoke Chinese, so we were something of a novelty. The locals would love to chat with us and very often they would walk us down the lane ways to show us properties.

At that time, most of the old buildings in Shanghai (and China) didn't have air conditioning, so everyone would sit outside. This was perfect for us: we could find a group of old women sitting outside which would be ideal because they would know *everything* that would be going on in the lane way. We would ask these women whether anyone had a house to rent or lease. We had started to build up a base of Western clients with money to spend on accommodation while they were in China and we would put the two together.

That was how we started and built our portfolio of property for rent. At one point we probably controlled about 80% of the ex-pat rentals in traditional properties in Shanghai, which is not bad in a city which on some measures is the largest in the world. With a computer, a desk, and two bicycles it was a pretty hand-to-mouth existence for a while, but the air conditioning came after three or four months.

We were lucky: we had chosen a very good niche. No one was doing what we were doing, and being foreigners in China, who spoke Chinese, was still quite a rarity which gave us a bit of an edge.

After some rapid growth the market changed, and changed both dramatically and quickly—competition got incredibly tight when so many people jumped into the market about 18 months after we started.

The difficulty with the initial business was that the barriers to entry were low—we started with a borrowed office, a computer, some bicycles, and plenty of bravado. To survive we had to upgrade and we had to put a lot more money into the business.

I always looked at SPACE as being a company that could generate enough money to keep a (basic) roof over our heads and to put (cheap) food in our mouths. But we never really looked at it as a business to make serious money. It was just a first step in building credibility and getting access to a network. It built the foundation to take a bigger step.

Moving into Property Investment

I always wanted to move into property investment, so I spent as little as I could and saved as much as possible. In 2001 the market in Shanghai opened up and sales of property to foreigners became legal. Before that foreigners were not allowed to buy property except in a handful of apartment blocks downtown.

It was all very new and no one knew how the system worked as nothing was written down, but prices were low and so I decided to take the plunge. To finance my purchase I had some money saved, I borrowed some money from home, and I got a bank loan. I got into the market at a very lucky time when the prices were very low. Since then the market has grown a lot.

At the same time we also wanted to get into sales. No one knew how property transactions worked, so the only way to really find out was to take the plunge and learn on the job. No one—even at the government department regulating property sales—knew how property transactions worked: there was no history of people buying and selling property as everything had been state owned. The real estate sales industry was literally taking its first faltering steps.

I sold the first property and made some money which I then reinvested in another property. I flipped properties for a while and this generated a reasonable income for a time, but it was not a business: I wanted to add value to those properties over and above buying smart and selling smart.

Property Development

Initially I just sold the property without doing anything, but then I started making some renovations to increase the value. By this time, through our real estate agency we had gained some experience with other properties in the city and so I had seen the best of the best. This allowed me to judge what was selling and what was leasing at this time, and what the standards were.

At this point the development business was my own sideline to the agency. With all the properties that I was buying and selling I got quite involved in the construction and the design of the properties.

Commercial Property

It was around this time that the residential market seemed to suddenly and dramatically top out, so we changed the focus to commercial property.

We couldn't compete with the big international commercial property brands which were focused on the large new commercial towers rising up all over China. I've always been passionate about the older buildings which have far more character and I felt protected from the competition if we focused on this niche.

There wasn't a way for us to get involved on a bigger scale so I looked into redeveloping old warehouse space into whatever the local market demanded and became one of the first Westerners in Shanghai to develop warehouse spaces.

Under Mao, Chinese cities had been split into lots of small to medium sized collective manufacturing hubs, normally with quite ornate warehouses in the middle which were now often in a state of disrepair. This pattern of warehouses was repeated across China from the center of the cities to the countryside. Typically we would rent these spaces for at least 15 to 20 years, then turn them into high-end creative loft offices and retail spaces.

At the same time, I still kept doing the old house renovations on my own. The commercial and warehouse properties allowed me to operate on a much larger scale. I started out converting a 400 square meter property, then a 1,000 square meter property, then a 5,000 square meter property (which is when I started working with my first development partner). I've now converted old factories including an old paintbrush factory, and there's also an old post office that I've worked on.

Growing Out of Real Estate: InnShanghai

In 2007, the residential market peaked, so we were looking at other ways to get more value out of the market.

We had foreign clients coming to town and they often asked us where they should stay. They knew that we could connect them with really cool property, so they figured we must know the really cool hotels. At that time there was nothing, so any time we had people coming out we put them in 1930s guest houses that were run by the government.

These were fascinating buildings which gave an experience like being transported to a period drama film set, but they weren't very high-end and weren't run very well. So we saw an opportunity to apply some of the skills and knowledge we had developed, but diversify into a different business.

My wife and I came up with the concept of trying to put together a boutique serviced apartment complex where each room was rented out for between two weeks to three months, and so InnShanghai was born.

InnShanghai has five rooms and is built within a 1930s French Concession downtown mansion. We gutted the building and rebuilt it with a mix of old furniture and hardwood floors. The finish is spectacular.

Learning a New Business

This project was great because it gave me the first taste of the marketing that is required for a hotel, the service that is required for guests, and the amount of work that is required in the hospitality industry. The business has nothing to do with real estate in any shape or form—it's pure service industry.

InnShanghai gave us a glimpse of that notion, but only a small taste. However, what InnShanghai did do for us was confirm that there is a market for what we wanted to do. It allowed us to get our head around the costs to design and build a hotel room. It also allowed us to start building our website and marketing platform. When moving on to the URBN hotel, my partner for the hotel and I took everything my wife and I had done with InnShanghai and upgraded it (significantly).

With InnShanghai, the construction was easy, especially as we didn't need any licensing, so we flew under the radar. The really tough part was managing the property without staff. For instance, we completely underestimated how much work is involved in making bookings. The sales side is tough and we had no idea about how much time was involved. But now we've got a full-time staff dealing with those issues in the same way that you would have for any normal hotel.

When we rented out InnShanghai to one company for three years I knew we had the concept for a successful hotel.

Moving into Hotels

By this point it was obvious that we had to grow out of straightforward real estate business because it was too simple. Too many people can jump in and flood the market, and ultimately there's a limited amount of income that can be generated from that sort of business. Also, the real estate fired me up less: I liked the construction and design side of the business.

So we started looking for a bigger space to do a 50 room hotel. I figured you need the same amount of administration and marketing for a 500 room hotel as you do for a five room hotel. Over the next year or 18 months I probably looked at over 150 buildings and negotiated on 25 to 30 of those. Four got close and failed, and the last one became the URBN hotel (urbnhotels.com).

All we needed was a shell so we looked at really poor-grade properties that we knew could be fixed up. As the Chinese have not had that much exposure to international design or aesthetics—partly due to the Cultural Revolution—they had little appreciation for architecture and interior design, so we found these great old buildings that could potentially become our hotel. In the end, we found a 1970s factory which was ideal. If we had taken any of the previous buildings we would have overpaid.

The construction side of InnShanghai was easy. By contrast, the construction side of URBN was highly complicated: we had structural issues and licensing was a nightmare. We were tested on every level.

As soon as we reached a certain size, things changed. We didn't get an incremental increase in complications; instead they increased exponentially. Also, when a business gets above a certain size you get known and all the bureaus will scrutinize you more closely. Other businesses will take your ideas more seriously and will try to replicate them (but, of course, at a lower cost and more quickly).

Becoming public in China is a double-edged sword. Halfway through the project we took our names off our website and any other publicity because as soon as people discovered that the hotel was owned and run by foreigners the price of everything rose and the apparent difficulty of everything also increased. We wouldn't have had those problems if we had been a local low-end hotel.

Learning How to Run a Hotel

I went through a lot of negotiations without winning any business and I am really thankful for that failure. If we had completed on any of the earlier properties, our business would have failed. It took us that long to figure out what we were doing.

While we were trying to find a suitable building for the hotel, we were also trying to build up our knowledge of the hotel industry, and in particular, the Western-owned boutique hotel industry (of which we were to be the first in Shanghai). More importantly, we were trying to work out what our costs would be: for instance, we had no idea how many people you need to run a hotel.

Our strength in business was negotiating and contracting, and this was coupled with a deep knowledge of the city and the market. We had background data from InnShanghai so we were not completely in the dark. But our fundamental problem with diversifying into a hotel was that we didn't know how a hotel works.

We spent a lot of time trying to meet hotel people and hotel management companies in an attempt to get any bit of knowledge that could be fed into our business model. Only in the last few months before we got what ended up being the property that became URBN did we get into the right frame of understanding to go forward.

The Business Case for Hotels

I knew that we had to grow and within the business we had a big debate about how to achieve that. When we found the property that became URBN, we had a long debate about whether we should turn the building into very high end office space which we could do with a very fast fit out, and without having to do much work, or whether we should create a hotel, which we knew would be much more service oriented. We didn't realize how service oriented it would be.

After a long time spent talking about it, we finally decided to go with the hotel because to grow as a business—and as people—we needed something that was sophisticated and which distinguished us on a design and service front. This was the only way we were ever going to get access to good real estate in Shanghai and was the only way we could create any sort of competitive advantage for us.

Anyone can put together a simple office: it's just not that complicated and for us, it was not interesting enough, or enough of a change from what we had done. It takes time and it takes a certain level of skill, but at the end of the day, it is a business that anyone who is moderately competent can get into. But my partner and I figured we had the design and the construction capability to be really ambitious. We love design and people, so we went with the hotel.

Running the Hotel

We both had management experience, but service is not our dying passion and so we looked for a hotel management company to help us run the hotel. However, there were none in Shanghai and no one seemed to have any idea how to set up such a business, particularly one to run a boutique hotel in Shanghai. This left us without a choice.

We had to grow into a more sophisticated business if we wanted to make a career and if we wanted to get into the larger scale developments. We wanted to make a quantum leap from doing average developments to doing larger development and/or more sophisticated forms of investment. To do this we really needed a showpiece development that shouted "hey—we can do this, we can bring all the pieces together".

Implications for Our Business

The hotel is a real Shanghai showpiece and has allowed us to take a real step forward which makes the trauma that we went through all worthwhile. It was worth every sleepless night.

The barriers to entry to the hotel business are very high. It is a very hard business to get into and to stay in. Ours is the kind of business that is comparatively unique in China. It's much harder to copy what we've done—and do it properly—than it is to copy a real estate agency or office development.

We believe that the Chinese understand the complexity of what we have done. Where they can look at an office complex and think "I can do that", they look at URBN with the sophisticated, well-executed design and they recognize that it is a complex business that would take a long time to understand. It is as close as we can get at the moment to a business that can't be copied.

People understand how difficult it is: a guy with money can't walk through the door and do it—they need knowledge too, and that knowledge is hard to come by and only comes with experience. I need to build on this experience for the next challenge and remain nimble for the next diversification I may need to engage in, whatever that may be.

Business Changes in China

The good thing about China is that the business environment moves very fast and the growth rate is high. The bad thing about China is that the business environment moves very fast and the growth rate is high.

In many ways my business could have been built in any major city anywhere in the world. The difference that China makes—apart from the opportunities offered by the phenomenal growth—is the speed of business change and the absolute necessity to change and keep changing. This is not simply a case of reviewing a business plan from time-to-time. Survival can mean tearing down your business and starting again at regular intervals and in my opinion, failure to reinvent your business when the environment around your business has changed can pretty much equate to failure-end-of-story in China.

Once you understand the basics of doing business in China—and do not underestimate that it will take a long time to acquire a rudimentary knowledge—the biggest risks come from what you don't do. In my experience, making a less-than-good decision in China often carries less risk than not making a decision when a decision is needed.

The End of SPACE: The Need to Change

Since the real estate agency was set up in 2000, I've had to change the business model every 18 months/two years because someone has picked up on an idea and copied it, or government regulations have changed, or there has been a change in the market.

I had a really strong property sales company for a while: the company was selling lots of old properties. Over the last three years taxes on property have been increased and there are also higher taxes if you sell within five years. Incredibly, this business has all but totally vanished. It took days to go from a significant size to nothing.

I kept the agency open for a long time, but I decided that the market had changed so much that it didn't make business sense to continue to run the business. Instead we are going to focus on property development and investment. The key staff have transferred from SPACE to SPACE Development (space-development.com) and I have licensed the SPACE brand, so I now no longer have any involvement in the running of that business.

It was a tough choice to walk away from the SPACE business because it was my first company and there is a lot of value attached to the brand. But it wasn't making sense as we would have to grow it in a way that we didn't want to if we were to stay in business. Our future now lies in areas that have more flexibility for us and which allow us to maintain flexibility.

For our future developments, we will also try to either work with a larger developer who has access to land/property where we can develop, or work with a government-related management company. On some level we will have to always work with a bigger partner in order that we can focus on doing business, not on sorting everything out before we can start business. Clearly there are risks of working with partners, but we should be able to work those out—it is preferable to have a business where you need to work things out, and are slightly less profitable, than to have no business.

This new approach will allow us to go into different types of property and in any location—this flexibility is something that we value highly since the business environment can change so much. It will also be less staff intensive.

Personal Drivers

In addition to the business reasons to close the agency, there were personal reasons. For me, there were no personal reasons to close the agency—emotionally, I would keep it open forever—but there are personal reasons to do other things. For me, everything has changed so quickly since we opened URBN.

In China everything changes very quickly and flexibility to cope with this change is important. I've already mentioned the business need for flexibility to stay competitive, but on a personal level, I need to stay flexible. China is where I want to live and where I choose to live, but I want that to remain my choice and not to have outside forces requiring me to stay here. I need the flexibility to be able to live and work anywhere else in the world that I choose.

The agency was very focused on a particular geographic location (Shanghai) and was very staff intensive. Both of these factors limited my flexibility. With the new direction, we can develop and invest in a location of our choosing—we don't have to be tied to one specific geography. As part of that, we will ensure that we outsource the more staff intensive parts of the business so that we can maintain our flexibility.

Also, the agency is much more of a mass-market business dealing with lots of individual customers who we usually work with once. With our new focus we will be building long-term close relationships with a much smaller number of businesses, and working together over a much longer period of time. The development side also gives us more creativity which we really enjoy.

It's really hard to get any traction with the mass-market businesses. With a relationship-based business, we are hopefully building life-long relationships and so we should be able to keep what we build. With mass market businesses, what you build can lose value very quickly. It gets tiring constantly having to reinvent the wheel.

For us, our business is becoming a lifestyle choice. We're making lots of decisions based on where we want to be and what we personally want to be doing. I don't want to be a pawn in the market.

Shrinking to Core?

In some ways it would appear that our new strategy is us shrinking to our core competence—in other words we are "un"-diversifying. While this is true in some ways, it's not really the story. While we now have a central focus—investment and development—which appears to be narrower, our diversification can be achieved by outsourcing, so we are keeping the diversification, but achieving it in a different manner.

The key for us is the theme that I've already mentioned several times: flexibility. With our new approach we can keep diversifying—we won't be tied down at any step and because we are a fundamentally smaller organization (albeit with more outsourced parts) we will be able to change more easily. We still have many skills and we can work in different areas such as residential or commercial and we don't need to employ specialist teams to maintain the different markets.

The development side is quite sophisticated and includes design, construction, marketing, and management. There's a lot in there and we're acting in a different way. Now we've got a lot of skills and a lot of contacts so we can market ourselves as a very broad-based company with a wide range of skills even though we now have less people.

We are still very adaptive. We do still have to work within the market that exists: if residential is on the up, we can go for that and if commercial is hot, we can jump in there. We can adapt to what is profitable, rather than trying to work in a sector that may have its margins squeezed.

Capitalizing on Confidence

For us, another reason to make the change now is to capitalize on the confidence that people have in us.

URBN hotel has garnered so much press coverage and has been mentioned by some publications as one of the top hot hotels in the world—we have been mentioned in over 600 international and local articles since the hotel opened. We have won six major awards: one of them was in the Condé Nast Traveler: Hot List Hotels 2008. We were also the runner up in a New York style award.

This coverage in newspapers and magazines has directly translated into confidence in us which has led to other people approaching us with offers. There are a lot of opportunities that we would now like to capitalize on and so we are hiring a business development person to help us follow up these opportunities.

Our offers are coming in different forms. Some international hotel companies have asked us to partner with them—perhaps they might take our brand and grow it and we have talked about growing the business in China with them. We have had discussions with hotel management companies and we have had talks with international real estate developers who would love to work with us either as a partner or an investor. People have also approached us with projects in China where they think we could help them and we've also been approached by people in China who have access to land and/or real estate and want us to help with the execution of their ideas. We've also had several approaches from people who are interested in buying the hotel.

All of these approaches make us realize that we made the right choice by building a hotel rather than an office.

We plan to open 10 more hotels in the next five years, but there are a lot of other opportunities: our next step is to understand those opportunities and choose the right ones to work with. The hard decision is what we don't do, rather than what we do choose to do.

China has no shortage of opportunities and many entrepreneurs in China have attention deficit disorder. We are not significantly different at the moment. However, I have just turned down some large and interesting projects—while these were great and interesting projects, and there is money to be made, we are trying to focus and some of the projects we have turned down would have distracted us.

With the Benefit of Hindsight

With the benefit of hindsight I can look back and ask those "if you knew then what you know now, how would you have acted differently?"-type questions. For me, the answer is simple: I would have got into development and investment five years ago, instead of trying to build a Shanghai-based staff intensive business.

With a staff intensive business, you become a manager looking after people, rather than a professional executing your business. It is great that we have the knowledge and experience that we built up over ten years because it makes us stronger when we analyze an investment opportunity, but we would have been a lot more profitable if we hadn't gone down this road.

I would also have got investment earlier on to move the business along much faster. Things move so quickly here and with investment we could have taken advantage of opportunities much more fully and more swiftly.

With investment we could have gained access to more land/property and would have been able to undertake bigger projects. The investments would have given us access to people who could become stakeholders and help us with our projects. Investment would have also allowed us to get away from the Chinese mentality of cheaper and faster, allowing us to focus on quality. That requires more investment and better partners.

Also, with some of the previous businesses, they were great, but they didn't have the right kind of scale to hire the right management. My strategy is now to work *on* our business, not *in* our business. To do that, you need to find the right people to run the business. Now we can set up the business and build it, not run the businesses as the management.

The Notion of Risk in China

In the West, lawyers are a bit like car mechanics: you present them with a problem, they suck their teeth and make a pained expression on their face, and you know they're not going to give you good news. However, China has far less of lawyer-based culture and so the nature of risk is considered in different terms, and you don't get that nasty disapproving look that immediately precedes a large bill.

In the West, the most serious risks that are usually considered are legal/contractual risks and the risk of ending up in litigation—that's not to suggest there aren't other significant risks: these are just the ones that take up the time. When you bring that orthodoxy to China, you find a lot of gray areas that need to be sorted before both parties can agree a contract. In my experience, the Chinese simply do not perceive that these issues could be viewed as risk.

In China, it is commonly accepted that you do business with your friends and as a result, many Chinese are happy to deal without a contract (indeed, most Chinese would probably prefer to deal without a contract).

For a business to grow in China there will always be a whole range of things that shouldn't be there if you take a conventional Western view of any deal. There is a lot of risk involved in doing business in China; however, one of the biggest risks is not being in the game. These risks are set off by great rewards and a fairly short gestation period for most businesses.

If you do get a contract, you will never get everything you want written down. The other side will always hold things back to keep power over you. If you don't want to make the deal on those terms, then someone else will take the deal. People are always willing to take that risk.

When we first started dealing with our landlords we spent time with them: we went out drinking with them, smoked their cigarettes, and had endless meals with them. We even got on the ground and arm-wrestled with them. We pretty much did the whole Chinese buddy-buddy thing and after this we felt there was a bit of a connection with them.

If we hadn't felt that connection we probably wouldn't have taken the risk. But these are two older ex-army guys—very much salt of the earth types—and we felt they gave us the deal because it was interesting to work with two young foreign guys who were both committed to working on the ground to make the business work. Also they felt that younger foreign guys wouldn't be able to screw them, so there was less risk from their perspective.

Both sides were right. We were able to befriend them on a level and they gave us what we wanted. We just had to go out and spend some time with them.

Because we understand the nature of the risks we are taking—and more importantly, we understand the nature of many perceived risks which are just low-level irritants, and we can minimize those risks—we're able to move in this market where a lot of people aren't because they don't understand the risks. We can quantify the financial implications of any risk we take and we have sufficient understanding of the culture out here to allow us to mitigate that risk.

To survive in China you need to constantly be growing your company. That's a basic business technique that is applicable the whole world over, but in China it is a fundamental survival strategy. You need to keep pushing the limit, and the moment that you become complacent, with the speed at which things change within this country, it means that everyone else will run right past you.

So you have to move quickly here. And if you're not already planning the next move and the move after that, then you're already too late.

The Fear Factor

As we've become more established, I've found a new fear: making a mistake. I'm not sure whether I've become more cautious, or if it's simply a matter that I understand more and so now I am more cautious.

I was recently looking at a project that is similar to URBN. It was twice the size, but it had some peculiarities that we were willing to work with. We negotiated for four or five months and were getting close to the contract stage but then we found some licensing issues. When I realized how vulnerable this project was—irrespective of how good the business model was—we pulled out due to these licensing issues. The government side, along with other risks, has to be recognized, appreciated, and addressed. We pulled out of the project because we can't afford to make those sorts of mistakes (again).

With a bigger project, with more investment and bigger costs, problems become more dramatic. So now we're looking to make sure our business model mitigates the main business risks. When we didn't have anything to lose, we were happy to go for it. Now we have a lot to lose and that makes us more cautious. That being said, I still think we're very aggressive in what we do—we're just always looking for better ways to do things.

Equally, now that we've proved ourselves, we don't need to take the risks to prove ourselves. Indeed, the converse probably applies: we have to continue to prove that we're not a risk to our partners.

Mistakes

If you're going to grow, diversify, *and* take risks, then you're going to make mistakes. The key is to recognize those mistakes (quickly), minimize their impact, and move on while learning any lessons.

I've made a million mistakes. Let me tell you about some of them.

Holding On For Too Long

I held on to a business that didn't have the room to grow. I should have got out of the real estate agency at one point and gone directly to property investment. However, I had spent so much time building the brand that there was a lot of emotional investment that influenced my decision too strongly. I got emotionally attached to my business which was a weakness. I didn't make a cold assessment based on its business merits (or otherwise).

This mistake has now been fixed.

Not Getting Investment

It was a mistake not to get investment in the beginning to grow the company. The market out here moves so quickly that I spent time earning money to grow the business rather than growing the business.

Partnering

I probably should have partnered here and there. I tried to do a lot on my own. Maybe it was a pride issue: I felt that if I could learn it on my own it would be better for me in the future.

Relying on the Wrong People

In the hotel we relied on people to help us with crucial parts of the project instead of building those resources internally. Part of that was out of fear that we didn't know what we were getting into.

We allowed our licensing to be controlled by a friend/ associate of our landlords, and we got taken for a ride. This individual didn't have the same need for the license that we did. Also, he didn't have the same time pressures that we had and he didn't have any incentive to achieve. In short, there was no risk on his shoulders.

Not Acquiring the Right Talent

There's a lot of fear whenever you have to deal with the government. Our fear allowed us to make a bad decision with the individual who was meant to help us with the licensing.

While we expended time and energy relying on the wrong people, this became time wasted twice. Not only did we waste our energies on the wrong person, but we didn't spend our time acquiring the right people in-house.

Taking our licensing example, you really need to have extremely trustworthy people when it comes to licensing and government relationships. We now understand that these people need to be in-house. We now understand that it's really dangerous to do business out here, especially a big project, without those types of people on your team.

But the licensing talent wasn't the only talent we had difficulty finding. We've been through two general managers for the hotel. This is down to a number of reasons:

- We didn't understand how to hire the right people in China.

- We didn't understand what we needed.

- China lacks good middle to high level management talent (in all fields).

It was tough for us opening up the hotel—there are many hotels in Shanghai, but at the time we started building, there were no boutique hotels. We hired a general manager of a 200/300 room Chinese hotel, a Malaysian guy who spoke Chinese and good English—we figured if you can handle that size of hotel, then 50 rooms must be easy. What we found was that our business model of a smaller boutique personalized service was not what he had been trained for, nor was it the kind of experience that he had been running.

He was used to having a huge staff to do everything for him. We put him in position before the hotel opened so he could help us with the set up which takes so much effort—the problem solving skills that required are phenomenal. There are 5 million ways to sharpen a pencil and no information is readily available.

We had a number of positions that needed people to do a lot of creative problem solving and found that most people we put into key positions didn't survive. If it needs to be done at a high level or in a competitive industry, then there aren't the skills available: there are so many moving parts and it's hard to find experts.

We made mistakes, but we did build and open the hotel in record time. Although we made mistakes, it has taught us a hugely valuable lesson. Next time we will spend more time, spend more money, and make more effort to find quality, experienced people to help with certain areas. We underestimated the difficulty of putting together a business like URBN. While we were individually capable of doing the work, there are only 24 hours in the day and our management team at the start was not capable of doing a good job.

So next time we'll hire head hunters who can help us find the right people. We'll only go with people with specific experience in this industry, preferably experience of the same size hotels. It sounds like common sense, but when it's so hard to find people with skills, we tended to think that we might as well take this person because we can't find anyone else. I don't think we would do that next time: we would rather slow the process down than hire the wrong people.

Lesson Learned

- As a basic operating principle, most businesses in China diversify. The common non-Chinese reason for diversification (that you will have different income streams to help balance out business fluctuations) is applicable in China, but is not the key motivator. Instead many businesses diversify so that if one enterprise gets closed down or fails there will still be others generating income.

- It is important to get the right people on board. If there is anything that is fundamental to the success of your business, then you should be relying on staff who are directly employed by you, with whom you have regular (ideally daily or hourly) contact so that they understand the issues. These people should have their rewards directly linked to the success of the business.

- As a corollary to the previous point, always create a business that can afford the right top management. If you don't, then you're going to be working in the business, not working on developing the business.

- It is critical to be able to move quickly. Often the risk of omission is far greater than any risk of commission. To move quickly you also need to be able to learn and you may need to learn how to accomplish tasks that may never have been done before.

- Do things that cannot be easily copied. The more complicated something is—the more you need to bring together a range of hard and soft skills—the more likely you are to be able to keep your unique market position.

- Find partners who are bigger than you. Ideally you want partners who have influence and who can flex a bit of muscle to cut through bureaucracy. A bigger partner will be able to watch your back and you will be less likely to be affected when smaller government bodies try to show how much power they have. This will stop individuals in small local bureaus from hurting your business.

- Take less ownership in exchange for strategic partnerships for financing and access.

- Make sure the business has the growth and scale potential.

- Everyone gets sucked into the China philosophy where things are so cheap. That is a dangerous mentality to maintain—you still need to pay for quality, but make sure you put money in the right places.

Chapter 8

Exploring the Road Less Traveled

Grace Liu is an ABC: an American-born Chinese. Both her parents were born in China but immigrated to the States where Grace was born and grew up.

After receiving her degree in Asian Studies at the University of Michigan, Grace went into the corporate world and worked for IBM's sales and marketing operation in New York. An opportunity to work in Hong Kong in 1990 saw her come to China. However, corporate life didn't fire her imagination in the same way that the creative arts did so Grace left to set up her own business.

Asianera started as a very small company in Hong Kong sourcing Chinese folk art and antique hand-knotted rugs. The company grew and one project required Grace to find a factory to make some hand-painted porcelain items. Although the project ended in near failure, it led to two changes which together laid the foundations for what was to become a highly successful business.

The first change was that Grace understood that she needed to set up her own factory in order to maintain quality and to give her the ability to implement her own designs. Second, it introduced her to Jian Ping Li (JP), the person who was to become her business partner.

Since that shaky start, Grace and JP have together built Asianera into an internationally recognized brand whose unique hand-painted porcelain is now seen on fashionable dinner tables, and in high-end shops and restaurants around the world.

By any stretch of the imagination, the way Asianera looks now is nowhere close to what I envisaged when I first started putting the business plan together. Like most businesses we evolved over time, and of course we continue to evolve. But evolving hasn't meant losing our original vision and values for the company.

My first business venture on my own was selling folk art and antique rugs to overseas galleries. This was something of a placeholder until I could really figure out how I could incorporate my passion for ceramic arts into a viable, sustainable business. Yet at the same time, I was getting my feet wet figuring the ins and outs of how to run a business on my own.

I was already very interested in ceramic arts as a personal hobby, but I understood the limitations of my own creativity and my limited capability to produce the ceramic pieces. I was passionate about both the creative process and the manufacturing process, and finally I got an opportunity to develop a line of hand-painted porcelain dishes for a client. That was the start of a huge adventure for me.

The purpose of starting my own business was never specifically just to make money, although, of course, any business has to make money in order to survive. However, over time, I was able to define what the vision for Asianera is:

1   Develop Asianera into a recognized Chinese brand which can have a positive force within China's porcelain industry in terms of creative design, high quality, and the preservation of the craft of hand-painted china.

2 Foster greater respect in the porcelain industry for creativity, intellectual property rights, ethical business practices, and social responsibility by endeavoring to be a business role model in these areas.

3 Develop Asianera into a platform to build cultural bridges and act as an incubator for creative collaborations.

The business now designs, manufactures, and wholesales Asianera branded fine bone china to exclusive retailers, high-end hotels, resorts, and restaurants around the world. Another sector of the business manufactures private label fine chinaware for leading international brands like Shanghai Tang and Alessi.

Setting up Asianera

When I decided to work with a factory, I didn't want to go to Guangzhou as everyone seemed to be going there and also, I don't speak Cantonese. Instead, I went north to Tangshan so that I could use the dialect I spoke. Through various contacts I found a producer who would undertake my project.

Choosing Tangshan

Tangshan, in Hebei province, is a city of about 3 million people and is situated 90 miles northeast of Beijing in the middle of a heavy industry corridor. In recent years Tangshan has seen a tremendous economic boom due to its well-established steel, coal, and cement industries which have been fed by the rapid development of infrastructure and the Chinese economy.

Tangshan is also known for its ceramics industry, particularly bone china manufacturing. Porcelain originated around the time of the Tang Dynasty (618-907 CE), but bone china was invented in England around the mid-1700s. The invention gave England a competitive advantage in the extremely lucrative porcelain trade. Bone china manufacturing only started in China during the 1970s with the establishment of China's first bone china factory in Tangshan, the Number 1 Porcelain Factory.

There are many ceramic centers in China, most notably Jingdezhen. But I chose Tangshan for a combination of reasons including, relative language advantage, already established contacts, relatively better infrastructure advantage over other areas, and proximity to a sea shipping port.

New Experiences

The experience of going into a heavily industrialized area which was not one of the main metropolitan regions, of going alone as a young woman, of going to areas where no English is spoken (my Mandarin was only mediocre at the time), was daunting. Although I put on a brave face and appeared to be Chinese, it was clear to everyone I met that I was a foreigner trying to find my way and this was all rather unusual at the time. There were risks, but it was a challenge that I wanted to take on.

This was 1994 and things were very different then: there were no highways in that area, only small local roads, many unpaved. My main method of long-distance travel was the train because it was very inexpensive, but it was often quite an ordeal. Since I was on a tight budget, I was staying in inexpensive hotels by myself. Needless to say, the experiences were all good character building exercises!! It was frustrating at times, but that was all part of the adventure.

One of my more memorable early experiences had to do with the Chinese language. English is my first language, and I had only started learning basic Mandarin in my late teens.

Mandarin is the standard dialect in China. There are hundreds of other local dialects in the country and some are so distinct from Mandarin that they are almost like a completely different language—for example Cantonese. Between these two extremes, other dialects have various degrees of similarities in word usage, intonation, and pronunciation.

Since Mandarin is taught as the national standard dialect in all schools throughout China, the majority of Chinese people can speak Mandarin, but most people have a natural tendency to prefer their own local dialect if given a choice. And in the less metropolitan areas of China, speaking standard Mandarin can be a chore for some. In which case, it can be extremely helpful if you know something of the local dialect.

I approached my first trips to Tangshan to set up my business with some confidence in my Mandarin skills but then I was so perplexed and frustrated during my first few days in Tangshan because I did not understand a good portion of what was said to me, and practically every sentence had to be repeated slowly. I was left wondering why I could not understand what sounded to me like Mandarin!

I realized that even Tangshan (which is less than 100 miles from Beijing) had its own dialect. Though not dramatically different from standard Mandarin, the Tangshan dialect often uses local words (not found in any Chinese-English dictionary) and different intonation. So for me, with a beginning-intermediate level of Mandarin proficiency at the time, it took quite a while to learn new words and get used to the local pronunciation. It was quite a revelation!

Finding a Business Partner

My biggest stroke of luck was running into my current business partner very early on.

Early in my start-up stage, I decided that it would be best if I could find a Chinese business partner. Though I am of Chinese heritage, I quickly realized that I was really more

American than Chinese, and the little I knew of Chinese culture didn't get me very far.

I met JP 14 years ago and we have been working together since then developing Asianera into what it is now. I had realized that it would be difficult to build the company on my own and that the best option would be to find a trustworthy partner—I was lucky to find JP: he was a godsend.

We met on one of my early trips when I was looking for a porcelain factory to undertake my first project. JP was the deputy manager at the very last factory that I visited and he was the only person who was willing to take on the project for me.

I spent three months working on the project, going to the factory every single day and managing the project with JP. This meant we were spending between 8 and 12 hours together every day, and so we got to know each other—and each other's working style—really well.

I realized that JP was a genuinely honest and sincere person who was also very artistically talented. The critical thing for me was to find a potential partner that I could trust and someone who I felt was a good person. JP fitted these criteria.

Although JP gave huge amounts of input, the project was actually quite a disaster (for reasons not related to JP). Vigilant as I tried to be at all times, I was very new to this industry, and I didn't realize that JP's boss, the general manager, was taking advantage of my inexperience. That one project ended up with product that was so inferior that I could not sell it to anyone. Let's just say that it was a huge learning experience for me.

This led me to the realization that I could not outsource the work that I needed to be done—I needed my own factory to keep control. As a result I decided to start my own factory, and I asked JP to be the factory manager. I told him about my goals and my vision, and he was on the same page as me. We discovered we saw eye-to-eye on many things.

Aside from JP's integrity and artistic talent, one of the greatest contributions that he brings is his local and industry connections. Unlike the more developed economies or even the more developed cities in China where you can search on the internet for virtually any source or information on a topic, in the second or third-tier Chinese cities, good reliable information is very hard to find.

Most things are still done the traditional way through connections and through word of mouth. For example, when we first started out we needed to find a factory space to rent. You couldn't just pick up the newspaper or search on the internet for vacancies (the internet was still in its infancy and although more local information has gone online recently, data is still basic and often unreliable). Through a great deal of inquiring among friends, acquaintances, and an ever-expanding network, we were able to locate an ideal space for our new operation.

Setting up the Factory

It is quite a step to go from being a person who contracts with a factory to produce some porcelain to owning, setting up, and running your own factory. When I set up the business, it took four or five year to get in the black. We didn't set the factory up over night—it was a very long, very slow process, and each step was very deliberate.

Initially the factory was a small workshop with a couple of small electric kilns and a few artists. We bought in the white ware and we painted it. Gradually over time we added on parts of the production process. Our approach is not uncommon when building a production facility.

But what I found most interesting—and one of the reasons that we built our own factory—was the process. I love seeing intangible concepts turn into beautiful tangible objects, and seeing a lump of mud turn into a thing of beauty. I also really enjoy being a part of the manufacturing process. This is one of the reasons why I find ceramic arts so fascinating. It also gives me the chance to (literally and figuratively) get my hands dirty.

One of the strengths that JP brought to the business was his practical knowledge. I didn't know anything about production equipment: I knew the basics about studio ceramic arts, but not the factory process, so when it came to production, I was entirely dependent on him.

Building the Business

When we only had the studio, I was building up the market and getting orders for hand-painted pieces from many customers. One customer wanted a particular shape that we could not feasibly source from anywhere, and so we had to either disappoint the customer or to make it ourselves. We realized that we could make some of the simple pieces and this first slip cast piece began our move from being a studio to being a manufacturer.

Although the notion was always at the back of our minds, we moved deeper into the manufacturing process, sooner than expected, through this specific market opportunity. By expanding into full manufacturing we were able to grow the business. As we designed and developed more new products, we took deliberate steps to add the relevant equipment to fill-out the production configuration. This, in essence, is the way the company grew.

When we started on the road to producing porcelain, it was important for us that we didn't just replicate what everyone else was doing, but that we create new designs and a porcelain product with a very high quality standard.

There was a lot of learning about porcelain for me, and every day since then has been a learning experience. But there was also a lot of learning for JP even though he had already been in the industry for some 10 years. His background was in product development, so his experience of dealing with every element of the process from the raw materials up made him an ideal person to help the business grow. Beyond that, if he didn't know something himself, then he knew where to go for information with his incredible network of contacts.

Defining the Market

I put my foot down and insisted that our market would be the high-end market. We had to produce high quality product with a clear high added-value element. I was convinced that this approach was the only way we could stay clear of the crush of competitors who were crowding the lower-end markets, despite the fact that we could see the road ahead was going to be very difficult.

There was a lot of trial and error to get to a satisfactory high level of quality. There were times that frustration was overwhelming and my partner and I had serious discussions about whether it was worthwhile to keep on with our dogged determination to produce high added-value product. In those early years, we were surrounded by a number of JP's friends who were doing a brisk business in very cheap low-quality mass-market hand-painted pottery.

There was so much pressure to jump on the bandwagon and do what they were doing. But within a couple years, the market was saturated with small operations copying each others' designs and undercutting each other on price because it was so easy to set up shop and produce. Needless to say, none of the businesses could sustain themselves in such a price war.

We took away with us a lesson which we always keep in mind. Bigger and cheaper may be the road everyone else has been taking, particularly in China, but it's not the road we should take if we plan to build a strong design brand.

We finally did manage to develop our product to a consistently high level of quality with a unique design style which incorporated a high-added value in the fine hand-painting element. In the process, we discovered that we had developed a nice little niche market for ourselves. And with that we got our biggest initial break which was landing Shanghai Tang (a leading international fashion brand with a home lifestyle line) as one of our clients.

In retrospect, it might have been easier to achieve this quality and consistency earlier if we had a larger sum of startup capital. We would then have been able to invest in a stronger technical team earlier on. But the reality was that we were on a tight budget, and we understood that budgetary considerations would constrain our speed of growth.

However, if we had secured extra investment earlier on, the pressure would have been even greater and we might have been pressured to make compromises. Because we didn't have any pressure from investors (we were self-financed), we were able to stick with our original vision.

Design

Asianera's style is a reflection of its founding partners who are a seamless fusion of Asian (more specifically Chinese) culture and strong Western influences. At its core, is the desire to preserve the craft of the finest quality hand-painted china which earned China such renown centuries ago. The concept is not to reproduce Chinese antiques, but instead to define a completely new Asian-influenced contemporary style uniquely Asianera which incorporates age-old hand-decorating techniques as well as newly developed techniques. As a result, Asianera developed a product mix which fits into its own unique niche market.

JP is our Creative Director and in this role is responsible for overseeing the development of our new product lines. We have spent many years working with and developing our artists' artistic and design skills, and they have become one of our greatest sources of pride. We now have a core creative team who work with JP to develop new patterns and shapes. In addition, I also contribute design ideas and develop new designs when I have flashes of inspiration.

Intellectual Property

Copyright is something I feel very strongly about. Years ago I saw some knock-offs of our designs in a really cheap market and it shocked me. I was shocked and disappointed, but JP thought it was great—to him this was recognition. In his mind once you get copied, you have arrived. After our initial reactions, we discussed whether we should take legal action, but it seemed that the financial return from taking legal action wasn't worth the time or money.

Those who copy Asianera designs and many other brands will find it very difficult to establish their own brand because they don't have the capability to distinguish themselves with a unique look which is the essence of branding. So instead of taking defensive action by suing, we would rather take an offensive strategy by constantly innovating and creating new designs so that we are always staying ahead of our competitors. It is a much more positive way of thinking.

Our products are copied in many different ways. Sometimes our hand-painted designs are reproduced by machine and other times they are reproduced by a hand-painting process. However, one key difference is that our hand-painted designs and the underlying porcelain are very high quality. Therefore, as yet, no one has been able to reproduce our level of quality. Today we feel confident that we will be able to maintain our competitive edge as long as we can maintain Asianera's brand recognition as one of innovation and creativity.

The Road Less Traveled

Over more recent years as our business with the hotel and restaurant industry has started to grow rapidly. We have frequently encountered requests from clients to copy designs from other well-known chinaware manufacturers. What a temptation it was to just take the sample and copy it. How easy that would be! And besides, doesn't everyone else do it? Well, we were never the ones to take the easy road.

From an ethical point of view, I have never felt right about copying. From a pride point of view, I felt (and still feel) that Chinese manufacturers especially should take a strong stance and demonstrate that we should not be asked to violate Intellectual Property Rights. From a business point of view, I saw an opportunity.

Our initial core competency when we were in our startup stage was our fine hand-painting skills. Over time, those artistic skills developed into strong design skills both two-dimensional and three-dimensional. So instead of accepting jobs to copy designs, we offered to custom-design new shapes and patterns for our hotel and restaurant clients as a free-of-charge added value option.

This custom-design service provided our clients with first-on-the-market new dinnerware designs for their restaurants. This was great for them because claiming anything new and unique catches people's attention. The ability to provide this unique service to our clients was great for us too because it was very difficult for our competitors (domestic and international) to compete with this.

The porcelain manufacturing industry is not a particularly fast-moving industry. It is essentially based on economies of scale and manufacturing efficiency. That means factories are large with mass-production facilities that can be unwieldy. Developing and then producing custom-made designs, particularly shapes, can be an extremely expensive exercise. Traditionally, chinaware manufacturers would develop a few core product line profiles, and stick to those shapes for decades, but vary the patterns on them every few years.

As our successes at winning bids over much bigger and more reputable chinaware brands or much cheaper Chinese manufacturers began to accumulate, we realized that we had something special. Not only could we provide good quality design service, but our factory was small enough and our production line configuration was sufficiently flexible to handle customized orders. So once again, our quality over quantity mantra was reconfirmed.

At the same time, with our ability to provide customized unique designs as an alternative to accepting requests to copy designs, we realized our clients valued us even more as a company with integrity. So our reputation for offering a custom design service, high quality, and business integrity preceded us, and has brought in many more high-value referrals. Before we even meet these new clients, they have already heard that we refuse copy requests, and that, they say, is one of the reasons why they have sought us as it is a clear reflection of a company's integrity.

From our simple beginnings, we took the hard road because it was always the road less traveled by our competitors. We didn't choose the hard road because it was difficult. We chose it because that road was the one that would differentiate us, our products, and our brand from all the others. Added to which, it was a much more interesting journey.

Artists

Artists are at the heart of our business. Of the 200 people we employ, about 40 are artists. To keep a supply of potential new artists we have started forming alliances with local art schools. It's good to hire students out of the colleges because they have stronger technical foundations, but we don't insist on this sort of formal education and we have some really talented, self-taught artists. Sometimes the self-taught artists are more creative, perhaps because they haven't been conditioned by the "rules" that some art schools feel compelled to impose on their students.

Wherever we get people from, there is still quite a long and involved training process since ceramic art is a highly specialized skill. Depending on an artist's basic skill, it can take at least six months to complete this training. It takes a lot of practice to learn how to paint lines and brush strokes which exude life and spirit rather than appear unsteady or lifeless.

Also it's important that the artistic spirit isn't lost when an artist is repeating the same design over-and-over again—there's a really fine line between being too mechanical in simply copying a design and making a work of art. This is a big challenge for us. We consciously need to keep watch that the artistry doesn't become robotic and that the artists don't lose the spirit of the artistry. Yet there is a difficulty because our customers expect a high level of precision. They want the delivered product to look like the samples they have seen.

This gives us a challenge on the marketing side. We have to make sure people understand that what they are buying are unique works of art and each one is necessarily different from each other. That is the added value that they are buying.

One of the really wonderful things about designing and producing beautiful porcelain is the knowledge that in one or two hundred years people will still be able to enjoy its beauty. Someone may be rummaging through an antique store (or whatever has replaced antique stores in one hundred years) and could find Asianera dinnerware. I love the idea that we are creating something that can be passed down through families and is more than simply a disposable commodity.

In this age of mass production, it is important to us that we play a part in preserving the ancient craft of hand painting on porcelain in China. We want to build a greater awareness of the value in the personal care and individual spirit which is reflected in the artistry of each hand-painted porcelain piece.

Evolution

Some of our factory equipment was second hand. We bought it from factories in Stoke-on-Trent (in the UK) which had closed down due to inefficiencies, high cost of manufacturing in the UK, and the inability to adapt quickly enough to a rapidly changing world economy.

When we went around Stoke we had a premonition about what could happen to us. We don't know whether this is something we can avoid, but we don't think it has to be that way.

My view is that the change doesn't have to be quite as dramatic as it has been. There might be consolidation, but I don't see that everything has to close completely. I believe the best factories will survive and this is what we aim to be.

I am surprised how many porcelain factories in China still don't understand that to compete on price alone becomes a no-win situation over time when competition turns into nothing but a price war. China is now competing against factories opening in Bangladesh, Vietnam, and other locations that are now much cheaper than China because wages here have gone up, and the government is beginning to enforce laws requiring improved work conditions including improved social benefits for employees.

I see a lot of factories that are grappling with inefficiency and poor management. Inefficiency is a big challenge for us and probably our most significant weakness. In order to achieve the quality that we demand, we end up being less efficient than I would like us to be.

A lot of it has to do with management style and quality of management. It's a never-ending learning cycle. We're all still learning and all still improving, and I think that process should never end.

Lessons Learned

- Business plans will evolve and ideas will build upon each other to form a more mature plan.

- If you really believe in a vision, stick to it. You can adjust your strategy, but don't lose the vision or your core values.

- A bigger investment allows you to do more and possibly helps to grow the business more quickly. But the benefit of starting with a smaller capital investment is less risk and possibly it allows you the time to take more deliberate steps towards growth without the pressure of answering to investors.

- Find your added value in order to stay ahead of your competition. As the competition catches up with you, keep developing new added value for your brand.

- If you're a manufacturer, you can't compete on price alone. Eventually there will be a lower cost manufacturer somewhere else. China will not be the lowest cost center of the world forever.

- Good, honest, hard-working, and trustworthy Chinese business partners do exist. You just need to go and find those people.

- Find and walk the road less traveled. It will help a great deal toward product and brand differentiation. And besides, it makes a much more interesting adventure.

Chapter 9

Resilience and Persistence

Henry Winter arrived in Hong Kong looking to get into the music business but found this tough as he had no music business experience. When he found that failure as an entrepreneur wouldn't count against him, he set up his own business looking to develop his experience.

Henry couldn't crack the music industry through conventional means so he started his own music marketing company: Groove Street. This evolved into an interactive agency which introduced some highly innovative business ideas including being the first agency to execute a text (SMS) message marketing campaign in China.

The business was good, but not scalable which made it vulnerable. To counter this Henry started the ultimate scalable business—Smart Club—a loyalty club. With Smart Club, Henry has moved beyond traditional loyalty club practices introducing many new and innovative ideas such as member tracking coupled with targeted advertising, a way for loyalty club members to meet up and for members to share information, and the first dating service to pay people to use their dating service.

As something of a loyalty program veteran, Henry is now focused on how to take the elements of the loyalty business and reorganize them to make a more valuable business. Currently this is leading him in the direction of regarding the business as a media business which helps retailers and brands connect with consumers in a targeted demographic. Coupled with that, Henry is looking at opportunities where a retailer or brand can partly pay for a media package with their product.

Henry has used his television appearances to methodically ensure that he raises the profile of Smart Club. During these appearances he is always keen to drive potential new members to the Smart Club website—indeed he once managed to mention SmartClub.com.cn six times on national television in the course of 10 minutes. He presents himself as the happy entrepreneur which clearly strikes a chord with the local audience.

While there have been many innovations, the business has had a bumpy ride, but few other businesses demonstrate so well, and in such practical terms, the necessity to be resilient and persistent in order to survive in China.

I wanted to get into the music business, perhaps by starting my own record company but I didn't have enough money. So instead I started trying to match record companies with advertisers with me in the middle taking a commission. This company was called Groove Street and was my first entrepreneurial venture.

It was an exciting adventure but I didn't get rich.

Groove Street

Groove Street was intended to be the place where music (and later where entertainment) meets marketing. Then in 1999 I read about this new thing called the internet and figured I should be making some money from this too. I wasn't quite sure what the business model should be, but I did know that it should include advertising, entertainment, and the internet.

I came up with the idea of creating websites for companies that had already spent a lot of money to sponsor something. So a beer company might spend a million dollars sponsoring a tennis tournament and I would show up and say "why don't you pay me $50,000 and I'll make a dedicated website so you can capture information about the people who can't make it to the tennis tournament?"

So Groove Street became an interactive agency and did well. It started in Hong Kong and a branch office was setup in Shanghai in January 2000. By the end of that year it was clear that the business in China was going to dwarf the business in Hong Kong. The revenue per project was the same, but there were more projects and the costs were one-quarter, and so at the end of 2001 I gave up on Hong Kong and moved to Shanghai. Unlike most entrepreneurs arriving in Shanghai, I already had a branch office in the city with 10 staff working in it, and the corner office was already waiting for me.

In 2001 and 2002 the company had some significant clients such as Heineken, McDonald's, Alcatel, Nike, Pepsi, and Lancome. The company was the most awarded interactive agency in China during that time, but then things started to change.

One of the agency's key strengths was its expatriate partners who were young, energetic, and willing to work for low wages. But as these individuals got older they wanted to buy apartments and cars, and they started to get married and have children. These people were now less willing to receive low wages and be part of an entrepreneurial adventure—instead they were looking for higher wages and more security.

The reason that the business existed, and the reason that the business was able to win competitive bids against the big players in the industry in head-to-head pitches, was that we gave the same quality as the big agencies because we had a group of ex-pats working as partners but we were getting paid a comparatively low salary. If we were to pay ourselves a full market salary, then Groove Street would have to raise its fees and this would make our price uncompetitive.

Reinventing the Loyalty Program

We realized that we did not have a solid company which could grow and pay the salaries that we needed. To be brutal, Groove Street wasn't a real business, so I started looking to create a new business which would be financially viable (while paying good salaries) and which would be scalable. And so the idea of a loyalty program was born.

The idea was to create a loyalty program where the company would own the membership and would have contracts with retailers, and when the members spent money at the retailers we would get paid. The process was set up to be highly automated so there would be machine-readers at the stores and points could be tracked online.

Smart Club was born in 2001. It then took time to build the website and the first member registered in November 2002, but the real start date was May 2004. This was the point at which the business achieved critical mass with its second significant partner after the Shanghai transportation card: McDonald's. In May 2004 Smart Club finished installing a system in every McDonald's in Shanghai and McDonald's did some promotion for the system.

Initial Loyalty Program Idea

With Groove Street we had already started working for Heineken to create a website where people who were interested in a sports event or a music event sponsored by Heineken could register online to find out what was going on and to get updates. With Smart Club we wanted to see whether we could extend this concept to sales.

The first step was SMS (text messages). Working with my colleagues at the time Barry Colman, Aymeric Fraise and Josh Perlman, Groove Street effectively invented SMS marketing—we conceived and executed the first text message marketing campaign in China for Heineken when they were sponsoring a tennis tournament where Andre Agassi was the star player.

The deal was if you were in a bar (which is where 98% of Heineken sales happen in China) and you bought 6 Heinekens, you would receive a scratch card which revealed a number that you SMS in, and then you won a chance to meet Agassi. For everyone who signed up, we sent back an SMS message inviting them to sign up on the website (where Heineken could get their details) and this would give another chance to meet Agassi.

We knew that anyone who sent in an SMS message would be a Heineken customer. This allowed us to link together purchasing behavior with website activity which got Heineken very excited and won us an award.

Heineken then asked whether they could offer a loyalty program for drinking their beer. I looked into this and came to several conclusions:

- The infrastructure of tracking what somebody buys is very expensive. Seriously, hugely expensive. One of the main challenges is that you need to have an identifier for the person, such as a membership card, and you need to issue a lot of those since only about one-tenth of the issued cards will be used.

- There is a big marketing expense just to remind people to carry the card. If people don't carry the card, or have some method of being easily identified, then the whole program will fall apart due to neglect.

- Then there is the marketing effort to raise the profile of the points. This is especially hard at the start of the project when there may not be many places where you can earn points or there is low public awareness of the program.

- The next problem was that Heineken couldn't afford this. Although a beer might cost 40 RMB in a bar, the bar takes 25 and the distributor takes 5, so Heineken would get 10 RMB for each beer sold. Out of the 10 that Heineken receives, they could perhaps afford to give 1 RMB as a loyalty reward. For the drinker who has just paid 40 RMB, 1 RMB reward didn't feel like much. This would mean people would have to drink health-damaging amounts of beer just to get a fairly cheap prize.

In addition, although Heineken were the originators of the idea, they had some concerns of their own. One of the biggest concerns was that they didn't want their brand to be associated with a loyalty program. They had worked hard to build a brand that was associated with great beer—they didn't want to dilute it by associating it with points, or to devalue it through any failures in a point program. Accordingly, they were keener on an external points program that they could use from time-to-time in connection with a specific event.

Anyway, it became clear that a Heineken points system wasn't going to work for a lot of reasons. As a result I figured that the approach should be:

- A coalition loyalty program—where several companies work together to allow their points to be aggregated. So as well as drinking beer, consumers could earn points by shopping in other stores or buying other products.

- If I was going to do this, I had to get over this whole card-issuing and advertising problem, because that would be a huge investment up front and one that I could not afford.

One Card for All

So I came up with the notion of using a membership card that people already have. All I had to do was find a card that was already in people's wallets for some other reason—and ideally one that they would be unlikely to forget—and then negotiate with that card company so that we could also use that card for the loyalty program.

The solution was the Octopus Card in Hong Kong, which is the most successful public transportation card anywhere in the world with 110% population coverage. I proposed the idea to the Octopus people and they liked it—their marketing and business development people thought it was a great idea. As a result, I spent almost all of 2001 meeting with them every few weeks to refine the proposal and working arrangements.

While the marketing and business development people loved the idea, the board of directors liked the idea but thought that it wasn't a top priority, and indeed, there probably were higher priorities for the business to address. After a year I was left with a fantastic proposal which could not be implemented.

So when I came to Shanghai in January 2002 that loyalty program linked with an existing card was on my mind. I worked my contacts and eventually got an introduction to the Shanghai public transportation card provider. When I sat down with them, naturally, my proposal was flawless because I had spent the previous 12 months perfecting it with the help of the Octopus people in Hong Kong. I already knew their business and the challenges they would face.

At this time, everyone in Hong Kong—everyone, including me and the Hong Kong Octopus people—regarded the mainland as the rather slow, rather simple country cousin. China was the place where you spent forever achieving nothing—the place where things are done in a slow, backwards, state-enterprise way. The place where it takes six weeks to order a notebook due to the Communist bureaucracy and so no business could possible get done.

The reality was the opposite. Six weeks after my first meeting with the Shanghai public transportation card company we signed the contract to be their exclusive points partner. They saw the benefit, they did some due diligence, and they did the deal.

The learning for me was that the slow country cousin was much faster than the city slicker—in fact, Shanghai was becoming the city slicker. Then when the city slicker saw that we were doing something with the country cousin, Hong Kong Octopus called us back and wanted to do a deal.

Doing Business with Global Players

The conventional wisdom behind loyalty programs is that you find at least one really big company to buy into your concept and give out your points instead of giving out their own points, and then any members of their existing programs get converted to become members of your new plan.

This works well if you have $100 million of investment and have a great track record. In these circumstances you can back up your reputation with the promise of lots of advertising. But if you're Henry, in a small office with a few other guys, and I go to see a supermarket or a mobile phone company and show them my plan, they always say the same thing: "oh you foreigners, you're so smart... oh what a great idea... why don't you go and sign up all of the other market leaders in all of the other market segments, and then we will join."

No one wants to be the first person to join.

We thought we had cracked this conundrum with McDonald's.

Market-Leading Innovation

The deal with McDonald's was that we would provide a system to reward, and therefore to track, all of their customers. Almost all of the consumers of McDonald's in Shanghai used the public transportation system, so all we had to do was put in a little box at each branch of McDonald's and those people could use their transportation card and earn points every time they went to McDonald's. The beauty of this idea was that people did not have to carry a separate loyalty card—instead they would be tracked with a card that they would already have to carry to get around the city.

So we built this awesome system that would allow people to be tracked. It would allow me to pick any one of McDonald's 60 outlets in Shanghai and pull up graphics to show:

- the consumers who go to that outlet

- on a specified day of the week, and

- at a certain time of the day.

I could then push another button and send all of those people a targeted email, perhaps saying "we haven't seen you for a week, why not drop by, we're offering double points today." The system then tracked to see whether people actually did come back, and they often did. For me, it felt like a great marketing tool in a relatively low-tech marketing city.

This was a very simple and straightforward way to show return on investment in advertising. To this day McDonald's still say it was the most advanced system they had anywhere in the world.

The deal we set up with McDonald's was that we would set up the system and run it with them for almost nothing because this deal could bring us a million new members. We could then send those million people somewhere else and that somewhere else would pay us good money. In return for setting up the system, McDonald's agreed to:

■ print tray mats to advertise the program (millions of tray mats)

■ set-up in-store promotion of the program, and

■ train every cashier about the program and ensure they reminded each customer to swipe their transportation card to get points.

That was the plan and it all looked great in May 2004 when we installed the technology into the outlets and launched with 800,000 tray mats telling people in Shanghai about us. But then it went downhill...

We would deal with a junior person in the Shanghai McDonald's marketing department who would report to a not so junior person, who would report eventually to the marketing director in Shanghai, who would report to the Shanghai general manager and the vice president of marketing in Greater China, based in Hong Kong. Both the VP and GM would then in turn report to the Greater China CEO.

Within six months of the launch, everyone in this chain was out.

There was a massive purge at McDonald's and everyone down the chain was out. Like the rest of China, people changed jobs quickly at McDonald's. The irony is that as a loyalty program we did not have loyalty from our partners— in retrospect this was clearly an issue that needed to be better managed when people and processes can change so quickly.

So we were left with a new team at McDonald's who knew nothing about our cooperation and who would not be getting any career credit if the arrangement went well. These people just saw us as a distraction when they wanted to focus on the Olympics. On hearing that there was a loyalty program, the new people assumed that this arrangement would send people to them, where McDonald's was intended to recruit people for Smart Club.

So McDonald's stopped. They stopped printing the tray mats, staff at the counters (who turn-over every three months) stopped telling people to scan their transportation passes, and promotion stopped completely. The net result was that instead of recruiting 50,000 people per month, we were recruiting 5,000.

Arbitration

We eventually came to the conclusion that this inactive relationship with McDonald's wasn't helping us, so we met with them. The meeting didn't do anything, so we sent them a legal letter. That had no result so we sent another, and then we sent a third. On the third letter they met with us and came back with a proposal that they would give us three months' promotion and that would be the end of the business relationship.

Our contract wasn't for three months' promotion: it was for ten times that, so we rejected the offer and McDonald's responded by terminating the contract. Our recourse was to settle the dispute by arbitration at the Shanghai International Arbitration Commission which was the forum to settle disputes that we had agreed in our contract.

For me, this arbitration was a first: the first time I had been in court (on either side), my first time of going through a formal arbitration process, and the first time I had been fighting a multinational company. My initial view is that the rules of the arbitration process were applied equally to both parties, but it was still not a pleasant process.

It was clear that under the contract McDonald's were required to give us promotion and they had not fulfilled this obligation: we had made the investment in equipment and installing the equipment, and McDonald's had not met their side of the deal. The only matter to be decided was how much we should be compensated for that breach.

In China there is no notion of punitive damages or of prospective economic loss, or even of real value—for instance, there is no notion of the value of promotion on the tray mats: whatever the value is, in my opinion it is certainly more than the physical production costs of the mats. I felt we lost both opportunity and the value of the marketing that McDonald's undertook to perform—for us there was immense value in having a cashier say "would you like points with that". The cost to McDonald's was zero, but the potential value to us was worth millions.

Instead the courts look at direct financial loss—in our case, they assessed the loss as being the cost of the failure to print some tray mats. There was no way to measure the lost revenue due to lack of in-store signage and promotion, and there was no way to asses the lost revenue since staff would not say "would you like points with that", and so both were ascribed a value of zero.

At our first arbitration meeting it became clear that the issue would be settled on tray mats. McDonald's clearly had not delivered the number of tray mats that were specified in the contract, so the discussion came down to placing a value on these. McDonald's starting point was to show how cheaply they could get these mats printed and suggested a low figure. By contrast we suggested a figure of $1 dollar for each of the 13 million tray mats that should have been distributed.

The arbitrator suggested that if we wanted the matter solved through arbitration, then his expectation was that the value of the financial loss would be in the region of RMB 1 million to RMB 2 million (between US $150,000 and $300,000). In the end McDonald's offered us a settlement of RMB 1.2 million. While this number wasn't huge, given that McDonald's had done nothing for us in the preceding 12 months, it wasn't the worst result.

Once the arbitrator had suggested a number, there was little negotiation. McDonald's suggested they would pay RMB 1 million and with some discussions we managed to push the amount to RMB 1.2 million.

As part of the negotiation/dispute we could have gone to the media and made an issue of the story. We could have portrayed it as the American Goliath fighting the Chinese David, in other words, the nasty foreign aggressor picking on the local company. However, we decided not to try that embarrassment tactic.

In retrospect, if we had adopted this approach, we would have got more money from McDonald's, and we would have received the money faster. There is no doubt in my mind that it would have increased our chances of getting a "better" settlement. However, I don't know what the long-term repercussions would have been. It is unclear how this would have damaged our brand and what effect it would have had on other potential partners who may have been less willing to work with us for fear of ending up in the courts or the press.

However, arbitration was preferable for both sides since it was much cheaper and much swifter: the time elapsed from us first submitting the case to arbitration until we received the financial settlement in our bank account was four months.

One thing I have learned from the process is that taking legal action gets results. If you have several people wanting money, the person that sends the legal letter may get your attention. However, the person who serves you with court papers is going to get your attention and action.

Creating Coalition Loyalty Plans

Unicom is the number two cell phone operator in China, having 10% or 15% of the market share (which is a pretty good market size given that we're talking about the world's largest cell phone market).

We were excited about the idea of working with Unicom, especially as they would convert existing Unicom points into Smart Points. For Unicom, offering Smart Points was something they could offer that was better than what was offered by the market dominant operator, China Mobile. Here was an arrangement that included some very big companies (such as McDonald's) but which would specifically exclude China Mobile.

Unicom has an operating subsidiary in each of the 57 Provinces in China, so I talked to the marketing department in charge of the points program of Shanghai Unicom which is a huge company in its own right with hundreds of million of dollars in sales. They thought the idea was great and arranged more meetings which led to meetings with the Operations department and the Finance department.

They didn't say no—some people wanted to do it—but the concept didn't get approved because some other people didn't want to do it, and it wasn't clear why they didn't want to do it. If they had just said "no" that would have been far easier, but they didn't—they just kept talking and talking. Perseverance is important when doing business in China but it is essential to learn when you are going round in circles.

What I was asking of them—to go from issuing their own points to issuing someone else's (our) points—was a monumentally complicated business process change which could lead to many unresolved issues and open questions such as what happens if the points are not redeemed: who gets to keep all this money?

It has been my experience in talking to most big companies in China that they don't say "no". Instead they just keep talking and inviting you back for two hour information sessions where we teach them about our industry and in the end nothing happens.

After a long time talking when nothing much had happened with Unicom, except us getting frustrated, we went back to first principles and reminded ourselves that the whole point of our proposition to Unicom was to allow people to combine their points from various loyalty arrangements. As Unicom already had their own points arrangement, we wondered whether we could simply convert Unicom Points into Smart Points—this would allow people to combine their points.

We put this to Unicom and they said "oh... you want to become a Prize Supplier?" This would mean that when people redeem points, Unicom deduct the points and pay the Prize Supplier. That was all we were really after and it turned out that they had a standard Prize Supplier contract available for us to sign.

In one step we had created a system for people to be able to swap their Unicom Points for Smart Points and we tried to do some promotions around that—usually we offered an additional benefit for making the change. We did some promotions with Unicom for a while and for several months we were Unicom's most redeemed prize.

The lesson for us here was finding another way to achieve the same goal, and we achieved a result which I didn't even know was an option. We had made our coalition loyalty program fit into a different format, in other words, Prize Supplier (making us the same as the firm that supplies coffee cups). By working with a business format that they already had we were able to make the approval process almost non-existent, because there was a company procedure already in place.

That was a huge breakthrough for us. So now, if we find any company that has a points system, we ask them if we can become a prize supplier so that their points can be converted into our points (in other words, our points become a prize that their points are redeemed for).

Changing and Evolving the Business Model

The challenge always was, and still is, how to provide value for members right now. Even with a coalition program where you can earn points in more than one place, it can still take far too long to get enough points to get a significant reward. This is the case with other well-established loyalty plans throughout the world.

So we asked ourselves what we could do to provide value for members immediately on the day they join—perhaps they only had the points we gave them for signing up or answering a survey. We also had the issue in the early days that we only had one large merchant (McDonald's) where you could earn points, and we needed to have something to give people the incentive to go to McDonald's to earn the points.

If we only had large prizes (such as cell phones and laptops), then people would do the sums and figure that the scheme wasn't worth their time.

Smart Friends

To answer this challenge we came up with a range of options. The first was to provide a way for members to meet each other since they have at least one thing in common: Smart Club. In order to match people for social or romantic needs you need to know their gender, their age, and their location, which is information that we already held about these people, and so setting up a friend-finding service was not a huge step.

Most of the major existing loyalty programs around the world were started before the internet age. They were all built from the ground up—technically and philosophically—on a one-way communication model (from the program center to each individual member). The concept that members could communicate among themselves was (literally) inconceivable before the internet. And therefore to date those other programs have not adapted and do not think that way.

For most friend-finding services, it's free to put your own listing online but then you pay to contact other people. With this approach we could charge a small number of points for one member to contact another, and members could gain a benefit from the service immediately. Added to which, the benefit would be valued far more by the point spender than it cost us to provide.

So Smart Friends was born.

Later we added the notion of virtual gifts—so if I thought a girl was hot, I could send her a flower which would live on her page for three days and then die. Again this would cost a few points. The key issue here is that the perceived value to the member of sending a flower to a hot girl would far exceed the equivalent monetary value of the points spent to send a flower. Equally, the cost to Smart Club of "sending" the flower would be far less than the value of the points spent.

But the idea didn't fly in practice. The next step was to become the first dating service to pay people to use their dating service. We started giving out points to people who used Smart Friends and each time someone contacted someone else, we gave out points.

While it might be an unusual approach, there is value for the business in giving away points for contacting people. The process of one member contacting another involves many steps including:

■   Going to the website.

■   Writing the email on the website.

- Sending the email.

- Going to the website to read the message.

In total, there were a potential of eight page views for one message. The cost of the points that we were giving out for the message could easily be made up by advertising at each step.

Perhaps the prime reason it wasn't successful was that it was one of ten things we were doing. If we had just focused on Smart Friends we probably would have developed a viable business as one of China's leading networking sites.

Because we were doing many other things—and unlike the companies that just focused solely on social networking, we only had a small amount of resources dedicated to the concept—we couldn't compete. We didn't have scale and the resources to do a good job.

That being said, this element of our business was significantly different to our competitors in this sector. I looked at one dating site that had one million members which dwarfed our 40,000 members. However, when I searched on this other site for women between the age of 18 and 25, in the Shanghai area, and with a picture, I found 50 individuals. By comparison, we had 20,000 women, in Shanghai, and with a picture, and all were verified by virtue of being members of the program.

Smart Talk: eBay for Non-Physical Items

This idea of Smart Talk also came from the notion of how to create value immediately.

I thought about a frequent flyer program—if I'm going to a strange city, then I want to know where to stay and where to eat, and there are probably people in the frequent flyer program who will be able to make suggestions. In short, there is the opportunity to create value for members by sharing information from other members, so we thought about creating a platform where any member can share information with another.

Initially I thought about restaurant reviews, but then I thought further, and considered the guy flipping burgers who wants to be a rock musician, but can't live the dream because there isn't a music industry in China due to piracy. I thought why not let him put his song online and people could pay him a few points to download the track. If he could get 10,000 or 20,000 people to pay him a few points, that equates to a healthy reward.

I could create a platform to exchange micro-amounts of value for non-physical items whether that be a restaurant review or a piece of art: the aim was to create an eBay-type service for non-physical items.

What I did find was that in the Pay to See It category, the most read article that made its author the richest, was The Confessions of a 21-Year-Old Virgin (male virgin) which I suspect was written by one of my staff. That kind of literature seemed to work, even though that was never what we intended to do.

Raising Money for the Business

Financing has been a real challenge for us and finances have come from the most unlikely of places. Equally, money has not come from places I expected it to come from.

Let me tell you about where I have raised money and some of the ways that I have fended off bankruptcy. So far, I think I have avoided this fate 38 times.

Investor Walking Away

We had an investor from September 2006 who put in a monthly allowance that allowed us to operate at a stable level.

It didn't allow us to do anything spectacular, but it kept us alive.

Over time this investor put in a lot of money—by September 2007, US $800,000 had been invested. Then the money that was due in early October didn't come. I initially presumed this was a delay. So I called them and got no answer. I sent an SMS and got no response. Emails went but never returned. I could get no response.

This continued through November and December. It took me months to realize that the investor was simply not coming back even after investing so much money. We were a couple of months in the hole by the time I realized what was happening and didn't have the money to pay salaries or the two or so months' outstanding supplier bills. Clearly this was a significant learning experience for me. Primarily, I learned that I had to stay on top of these issues—I couldn't simply accept that money would be late.

A couple of staff filed legal complaints against us, another company filed a complaint against us and our Business Operation Certificate was temporarily suspended. Our invoice book (in other words, our source of income) was taken away by the government so we couldn't send out bills.

Technically we were insolvent and I was looking at a phenomenally messy and ugly ending where a lot of people would get hurt.

To make things worse, this was happening while I was participating in Win In China (which is the Chinese version of The Apprentice). So while my business was falling apart I was traveling to Beijing and spending extended periods of time there which made the whole situation more fraught.

To compound matters from a personal perspective, I also had a trip to Europe planned to meet up with my family. My girlfriend was coming and had a (quite reasonable) expectation of being proposed to during the trip. So at a time when the company was going down, I personally needed to raise money for the trip and a rather important diamond ring.

There were no investors on the horizon and no white knights to be found. There was no plan B. Things were going wrong so I met with the local managing director of a software startup company which we had been working with to help them create the first implementation of their software. I told them that they might want to look for other partners as our outlook was dire.

This small company's founder took an interest because their new business was based so strongly on working with us. Indeed, their relationship with us was the key part of the basis on which they were trying to raise funding.

So we came to an arrangement that they would give us $500,000 to stabilize the company and when they went to raise capital, instead of asking for $10 million, they would ask for $12 million. They would then invest the additional $2 million into our business in return for a controlling interest. It wasn't everything that I wanted, but at that point I had few options.

In the end the investor ran out of money and failed to raise money for themselves.

Chief Operating Officer and Losing VCs

In 2005 I was in negotiations with a well-known Silicon Valley VC firm. At the time I had a very strong chief operating officer. On paper he was the perfect compliment to me: I'm white, he was Chinese; I'm an entrepreneur, he had huge amounts of corporate experience; and so on. He looked like a great fit and the investors loved the idea.

This guy saved the company two or three times by first investing, then by taking no salary, then by loaning the company money, and then by persuading his friends to invest their money. He was responsible for about US$400,000 of cash flowing into the company over a period of about a year or so.

As a result of his generosity/commitment, our COO's personal financial status went from comfortable to not so comfortable. He went from earning US$250,000 a year and living in a comfortable house, to earning nothing and putting his savings into the company.

When we found this VC investment, we were finally going to get a salary and we had to decide on the number. Remember, this is China where getting US$5,000 per month is already a very high salary by local standards. With this level of salary, investors would rightly ask why there was a foreigner getting paid so much when a cheaper local could be hired.

Nonetheless, the Silicon Valley VC actively suggested that it was important to keep both me and the COO happy and comfortable, so we should both get $10,000 per month. This would have represented the highest COO salary that I have ever heard of for a business in such an early stage.

I was ecstatic—this represented a substantial salary increase for me and with my stock in the company, it looked like we were heading for the big time. Unfortunately the COO didn't see things that way. He saw that the company would be well-funded which would give his shares a certain value but that he probably wouldn't get any new significant new shares after that. He also saw that his salary was $120,000 a year where if he went back to his old company (or similar) he might be earning $300,000 a year (or more).

For him it was an easy economic decision and so he told me that he had decided to quit unless I gave him a lot more shares than we had originally agreed. I was not keen on his idea—we had a deal by which he would own 10% of the company but it would be hugely damaging to the company if he walked.

However, the COO was adamant: he had two options—by one he made $120,000 and by the other he made $300,000. The only way he could see would be if we did something to change the equation...

I weighed up the pros, the cons, the in, the outs, the legal, the moral, the ethical, and any other aspect I could think of and decided to agree. The COO named a revised equity stake and we made the deal.

We had peace in our time... naturally, I was Neville Chamberlain. Within a week the COO called for another meeting. He had decided that the extra value for the "small" amount of stock that we had agreed was not right. He wanted more. I gave in. I gave in three times. Each time I asked what he wanted and gave it to him.

By the fourth time I realized that the process was never going to end. It wasn't a question of a mathematical calculation, but rather a matter that in his heart the COO felt that he wasn't getting the best deal. He would always believe that there should be a way for him to get both a higher salary and more equity, and in many ways this reflects the greed that some individuals in China can show. In short, he would *never* be happy with our deal—he would always want more money *today* and was not interested in how we could earn even more money tomorrow. So this was the point at which I said no and the COO decided to quit.

Clearly I had to tell the investors that the COO had quit. I called them and they freaked out and decided that they didn't want to proceed with the deal.

The Next COO
We were lacking a COO and a business partner recommended someone to us. This went wrong too, but much faster, and this second COO didn't put in $400,000.

We needed a COO and the CEO of a website that we partnered with recommended someone who was the head of business development for one of the top Chinese internet companies which was listed on NASDAQ. I was so grateful— we were in a horrible situation and needed someone quickly. And here we had someone local who came with a personal recommendation—he was clearly a guy who knew how to make things happen in China.

I talked to the prospect on the phone and subsequently met him. He seemed to have quite a nerdy/geeky kind of style (or lack of style), but his style was irrelevant if he was someone who would deliver. However, for the second time, it seemed a good thing to have someone to balance my more flamboyant, outgoing style.

Based almost entirely on the recommendation I hired this guy and made him a director, and made the deal for him to earn a significant equity share.

Very quickly it became apparent that he was not the right guy. Interaction with other staff—which he claimed was one of his strengths—was worrying. He said things that sounded silly to me and I later found sounded silly to my colleges: he would brag about how many dumplings he would eat at lunch. I thought this might be a Chinese thing... I later found that it is not.

He accepted projects—projects that should fully utilize his skills—such as redesigning our website, and agreed a deadline. The deadline came and it became clear that he hadn't started to do anything. This was a month long project which was critical to the success of the business. He had done nothing and didn't tell me about his inactivity until I asked him one day before the deadline.

I expressed my extreme discontent and he responded by saying that he had some personal business and needed to return to his home in Beijing. Very soon he stopped answering emails, he didn't respond to phone calls—he just disappeared.

Some time later someone said they had seen him working for another company in Hong Kong, but they had no proof. We heard, and have continued to hear, nothing. We sent him a legal termination notice and we received no response.

People

A key factor in all of my triumphs and tribulations has been the people around me.

Loyalty

To counter the shortcomings of people who have been at the company and who have failed to deliver, we have many loyal staff and many people who have left and are now at other companies who try to bring us business, even though they own no shares in the company and even when we occasionally owed them back salary or welfare.

They presumably do this because, apart from the financial side, they did have a very good experience of working with us. We took the time to train them and create a good office atmosphere. We treated these people—as we treat all of our people—with respect and friendship, and for most of them gave them a real opportunity to get involved with management or business development. Many of these people have had their good work at Smart Club recognized and have gone on to find great new positions.

I believe that treating people properly and creating a good team atmosphere has engendered loyalty in many people who have worked with us. A great example of loyalty came with the 38th (and most recent) saving of Smart Club.

The white knight that had saved Smart Club at the end of 2007 was unable to raise the capital that it regarded as already raised and was therefore also unable to raise the capital it promised to invest in Smart Club. Accordingly, that company was struggling to stay afloat and so, quite understandably, they didn't want to put their highly limited finances into a loyalty card program that wasn't part of their core business. In short, they misrepresented their finances and then breached their contract by which they would invest in us.

Then came Stanley. Stanley is a Taiwanese guy who had been with us for two years until the end of last year when he quit. When he left he was quite open and honest that he needed more money and our sometimes erratic payment of salary did not make family life easy for him. He needed a stable job with a stable company. He was so open and honest about what was happening that I couldn't be angry, even though he was leaving and taking a large chunk of our intellectual capital with him, which would be directly applied in his new company that was going to compete with us.

Stanley's new company had been set up by one of China's largest media groups: Xinhua Media, which is a huge conglomerate. The branch that owned Stanley's company publishes three of the most successful newspapers in Shanghai and some magazines. This group had decided that, since it had unsold advertising space, it could start up some businesses that would find print media promotion highly valuable.

The first business they set up was a car insurance business which they promoted like crazy and is now doing very well. Then someone pointed out that a lot of banks, telephone companies, and department stores advertise in the newspaper, so why not set up a loyalty card business to help these advertisers that they already knew? They set up their company to do that, and as part of this, hired Stanley.

However, progress was slow because they weren't sure about what they were doing. So when I talked to Stanley it seemed that:

- they had cash and promotional media, while

- we had experience in the business and a well-established brand.

Stanley spoke to some people in his business and we all met. Within three weeks a deal had been done and the Xinhua Media loyalty program guys moved into our office and I'm now running the business. They have paid our bills and we have enough money to run the business to the end of the year and an expectation of a further injection at that point. This means we can focus on running the business for the benefit of the membership. In addition they are providing huge amounts of media space to promote Smart Club.

As you might expect, my equity in this re-born company is less than it was before, but the benefits are so great that I think it is a good deal. Not only do we have cash in the bank, but we also have people at the media company looking to help us. One tangible result of this is that we have been able to use their relationships with the banks (because the banks do so much advertising) to negotiate a co-branded credit card with one of those banks. This co-branding with a large financial institution is the aspiration of every loyalty card program.

If I had pitched this deal directly to Xinhua Media they probably wouldn't have gone for it. However, because I was able to approach the deal in a very Chinese way—building and maintaining relationships (guanxi) and not burning my bridges—I managed to find the ideal deal, and a deal that I hadn't even known was available when I started the conversation.

Media and Entrepreneurial Philosophy

My work philosophy is that I want to build a comfortable environment for myself so I can do what I want to do, when I want to, and how I want to. By the same token, I feel strongly driven and bound by that same philosophy that it is my job to get publicity for the company and to raise its profile. That is my role and if I don't do it to the absolute limit of my abilities, then I am violating the code by which I work for a comfortable environment.

My approach as an entrepreneur makes me different to most entrepreneurs who will want financial stability as their number one priority. Once that is sorted, then they will look for personal happiness. I respect that approach, but it isn't mine: think what a waste it would be if aliens attack tomorrow.

My approach is to delegate the dull and uninteresting things to other people—I don't wait until I can afford to do it, I delegate now—and then I keep hold of the interesting things that I want to do and call that my job. I've also made sure that the office is set up in a way that is convenient to me—it's comfortable and it's just across the street from where I live.

This might sound ridiculous—and it is, if your measure of success is money—but my measure of success is happiness and so on my criteria for success, I'm doing the right thing.

Win In China

I took part in Win In China, which is like a Chinese version of The Apprentice, to raise the profile of Smart Club. Win In China is on national television and you are competing for millions in venture capital funding, so it really is a big deal. I was one of the most popular contestants at the point that I was eliminated.

For the Win In China interview I went to a juice factory about an hour outside of Shanghai. There were 100 people each day and three people would be chosen. There was a notice suggesting that everyone should wear a dark business suit. The other 99 did—I wore my red pants, red shirt, and a Superman belt buckle and took giant red cell phone. As I walked in the room, I saw the immediate shock on every face as they realized the inevitable conclusion that there were only two places left.

In the round before the finals began, there were 36 contestants who would be whittled down to 12. The format was a TV game show where you got to make a speech and answer questions. The speech was about you and your company, and the questions were about you and your company. It was a fantastic platform to talk about Smart Club.

Ignoring the judges' panel I looked directly into the camera and pitched Smart Club, carefully describing the business and the member value. The key judge said that this was the best company description—ever—in the entire three year history of the show.

I won that show and as the winner, I got one minute at the end to thank everybody, and so I used the opportunity to thank, and propose to, my lovely girlfriend on national television—the first time this had ever happened in China. This is now available as part of the box set DVD.

I reached the finals. This is where the 12 finalists live together in serviced apartments in Beijing and every four or five days we had to complete a task. The first task was to sell business to business internet services to key wholesalers. The second task was selling men's skin care products in a Beijing department store. The third task—where I crashed and burned—was to make posters for a men's fashion brand that wanted to be the Armani of China.

The show required that we wear the same outfit for the briefing and the final judging in every task, and we were not allowed to have our companies logo too prominently displayed. So I wore a very cool white Chinese suit where the other contestants all wore boring Western suits.

During the earlier tasks there had been no opportunity to talk about Smart Club and when we were doing the task we often had to wear some sort of clothing related to the product we were marketing, so I couldn't wear Smart Club clothing. But I was away from the business and living in Beijing—and at this time the business was in serious financial trouble—and I was doing nothing to promote the business even though I was still getting paid.

I felt terrible. I was betraying all of my principles.

With the third task, the brand we were promoting asked us to make posters of ourselves modeling the brand's clothes. We had to combine the Olympics, the brand values of being the Armani of China, and the spirit of the show. When I heard that I knew my moment had come—I could create a poster of Henry the entrepreneur; Henry the CEO of Smart Club.

If I didn't promote Smart Club on this task, I would be doing the brand a disservice and would just look like a foreign model. It seemed to me that by promoting Smart Club I would make the poster cool *and* I would promote my company.

When the day of the shoot came, I took a prop: an old-fashioned (in other words, large) mobile phone covered with Smart Club stickers. My idea was when there was to be a photo of me on my own, I wanted the prop in the photo. My team leader wasn't so keen—no one else had a prop or anything else to promote their company.

The argument that followed led to my departure. I am proud that I was kicked off for being loyal to my company. I am also proud that I was able to dress in a highly outlandish manner and able to draw attention to the Smart Club website.

The more outlandish my dress, the more hits there were to the website. Most of the other competitors just brought one nasty black suit where I spent a month planning my wardrobe so that I would get more air time, so more people would look me up and I would get more website hits for Smart Club.

Lessons Learned

- Take the money, then renegotiate! All valuable business partnerships evolve over time, based on the changing value that the parties can bring to the table. If the other side offers to buy, and won't budge from their price—SELL! If you really *are* worth more, they will realize they need additional service/help and will be willing to pay a fair price for it. This applies to getting work from big clients, and getting cash from investors. Don't get stuck on price, get the deal done!

- To get investment, you need a bidding war, no matter how low the bidding starts. Investors need motivation to pull the trigger and wire the money NOW. No amount of spreadsheets or business plans can supply that sharp poke. Calling an investor to say "I'm just calling to say goodbye"—while you are still thinking, "we're selling to someone else"—now THAT gets a dramatic and immediate reaction, no matter how absurdly low the price "someone else" may be offering.

- WATCH OUT!! Intelligent people (and anyone reading this book is surely in that category) naturally dislike repetitive simple things. Anyone for an all-night match of Tic Tac Toe? No—we invented chess and World of Warcraft to stimulate our minds. *Intelligent people naturally seek to make things more complicated* which equates to *more interesting work*. But companies get rich doing the same thing, over and over.

■ I treat all "work"—especially my full-time day job—as one of several "projects" that I am working on. This way setbacks are not so painful (as it will be only one of several projects... there will always be other flowers in the garden). Also, I only let myself focus on three key things per project (because I have to get on to the other projects—this ensures I don't have the time to get lost doing 10 key things on one project).

Made it in China: the Featured Entrepreneurs

M ade it in China looks at the experiences of a group of non-Chinese entrepreneurs who have all (individually) been highly successful in China. These are people who have gone to China, invested their own money, got their hands dirty, and have achieved. These are people who bring a "can do" attitude to their work and understand how to take advantage of the opportunities in China.

We are grateful to all of the entrepreneurs who have shared their experiences with us. Here's some further background about these people.

Bob Boyce

Montana native Bob Boyce is the founder and CEO of Blue Horizon Hospitality Group (BHHG), a company that owns blue frog and KABB, a family of bars and restaurants.

Bob always had a fascination with Asia, especially after a summer in Japan through a cultural exchange program at the age of 16. In 1994, Bob graduated from Northern Arizona University (NAU) with a degree in Communications, and decided to go to Beijing through NAU's scholarship program with the Beijing Second Foreign Language Institute. This gave him the opportunity to learn about China at a time when the country was just coming onto people's radar screens. Even at that time, China was a place with huge potential for adventure.

During the first year-and-a-half of his Chinese studies, he took the opportunity to explore China and to really get to know the country. The experience helped him land his first job as a sales manager for a relocations company, working in Guangzhou and then in Shanghai. The job gave him a firm basis for understanding the nuts and bolts of how to successfully run a business in China.

Since most of Bob's clients were foreigners moving into the Chinese market, they often complained about the lack of good places to eat and drink—especially places that served up Western style dishes with a relaxed atmosphere and good service to match.

In 1999, Bob decided to take a leap and start his own business. He set out to fill the Western food void by offering great quality, classic Western food at reasonable prices. His passion for building a locally grown brand and the company's service-minded approach to customers has helped distinguish BHHG as a market leader in the Western restaurants and bar scene in China. Today, BHHG oversees eleven restaurants and bars spread throughout Shanghai, Macao, and Beijing, and will open three more in 2009. The company employs over six hundred people from all over China and the rest of the world.

Bob is one of a handful of Western business pioneers in China. He is an active member of YPO (Young Presidents Organization) and the former president of Shanghai's Young Entrepreneurs Organization. He is also a frequent speaker on business and entrepreneurship in China.

He currently lives in Shanghai but maintains roots in Montana and returns frequently. The contrast between Montana's wide open spaces and China's energy offer him the best of both worlds.

Scott Barrack

Scott Barrack is the managing director and co-founder of SPACE: a business that now incorporates URBN Hotels and Resorts, SPACE Development, and SPACE boutique real estate agency. SPACE specializes in sustainable development and property/hotel management.

SPACE Development (space-development.com) is a sustainable development company specializing in the redevelopment and management of boutique and luxury real estate projects. SPACE (space.sh.cn) is a boutique real estate agency specializing in the leasing, sales, and rehabilitation of colonial buildings in Shanghai's French Concession. The award winning URBN Hotels and Resorts (urbnhotels.com) was one of Shanghai's first boutique hotels and is China's first carbon neutral hotel group.

Scott grew up on the sunny beaches of Newport Beach, California and the snowy slopes of Aspen Colorado with his two younger sisters and younger brother. After studying business at Arizona State University, his boyish dreams for adventure and opportunity landed him in the then lawless and newly re-opened China in the summer of 1998 when he was 22. Scott studied Chinese at two of China's premier language Schools—Beijing Language and Cultural University, and Dalian Language and Cultural University—and is now fluent in Chinese. He conducts the majority of his business negations in Mandarin.

Scott has a strong family background of entrepreneurs. From his earliest memories he dreamed of becoming a business man in a foreign country where he could play out his James Bond alter ego with exotic beauties, martinis, and lots of money—all in a foreign language that he only heard mentioned in cold war novels. Aside from the childhood lemonade stands, obligatory summer landscaping jobs, Scott's working career started in China when he worked in business development and sales roles in several companies before he started his real estate career.

In 2000, Scott co-founded his first company SPACE, a boutique real estate agency, with about US $500. He quickly bought out his first partner and began to grow the company. As one of the pioneers of the Shanghai real estate market, Scott became one of the first Westerners to start redeveloping the 1920/30s colonial buildings and became known as Shanghai's French Concession specialist. SPACE was awarded CNBC's 2008 Best Real Estate Agency in China.

SPACE, the agency, was the stepping stone and platform that Scott used to grow his development business. Starting with residential rehabilitations, Scott rapidly expanded his ventures to become a pioneer in creative warehouse redevelopment and then boutique hotels.

In 2004 Scott converted his first factory space into a mixed-use building and then in 2005 he opened Shanghai's first boutique serviced apartment complex, InnShanghai (innshanghai.com). Today Scott is engaged in over 20 development projects and employs over 150 staff. In the last five years he has moved over 15 times while fixing up houses then renting them.

Scott lives with his wife Jennifer and their new daughter Savannah Star Barrack. Savannah is by far his favorite creation and project to date. In addition to fixing up houses, Scott enjoys traveling, spicy food, and adventure. He is also an active proponent of the sustainable development movement and regularly speaks on green/sustainable development issues.

Graham Jeal

Graham Jeal is the founder and CEO of the Euro China Consulting group of companies (eurochinaconsulting.com) which includes investment, business finance, property management, and sourcing businesses.

Graham was born in Nottingham, UK and after reading Politics at the University of Durham worked with JPMorgan in London, New York, Hong Kong, and Tokyo. While at JPMorgan, Graham and his future business partner established the London new starters integration committee, signing off a cool US $200,000 to help "integrate" new hires in the London European HQ.

Graham has been thinking about and running businesses for as long as he can remember: he won a business plan prize at school, established a student newspaper at university, and ran a dot com while employed at JPMorgan. A free flight to Shanghai opened his eyes to a once-in-a-lifetime opportunity to be present at the birth of an economic giant. A second trip to Shanghai (paid for this time) resulted in the purchase of a property (on his 12th full business day in Shanghai).

After enduring ridicule, then interest, then enthusiasm for buying a property in China, Graham co-founded Shanghai Vision to help others make similar investments. Shanghai Vision set up offices in London, Shanghai, Dublin, and Sydney and had partner arrangements in the Middle East and South Africa. The company attracted over 500 property investors from around the world and built over US $200 million of assets under management.

While his business partner grew the investor base through offices around the world, Graham developed the Shanghai headquarters. In 2005 he established Shanghai Vision Asset Management to provide professional, and ultimately award winning, property investor reporting to Shanghai Vision investors. Graham exited Shanghai Vision and Shanghai Vision Asset Management through a management buy-out in 2007.

Today, Graham is a director of property investment and trading companies in Japan, Hong Kong, UK, Central Asia, and the Czech Republic. In 2007/2008 he was the President of the Entrepreneur Organization in Shanghai. He is a regular speaker at business forums in China and commentator on subjects involving business in China.

Graham lives in Shanghai and enjoys travelling, discussing business, music, and watching Nottingham Forest. When he is not travelling between the UK and China, he is working with a foundation he co-founded: Tomorrow's Entrepreneurs, an organization that supports initiatives promoting entrepreneurial education.

J C Lim

JC is the founder of several successful businesses across Asia.

He was born in Kuala Lumpur, Malaysia and had his first entrepreneurial experience while in high school. Challenged with raising money for a new school building, he organized a series of Tea Dances at local discotheques. This was the first time JC was involved direct sales and the venture was so successful that he raised one of the highest amounts for the school building fund.

After a traditional Malaysian education, JC studied Accounting and Finance at Macquarie University in Sydney, Australia. Life in Sydney on a limited budget was hard for a

JC who was forced to work in the Sydney fish market to make ends meet.

He began his working life as a junior auditor in Malaysia. A turning point came when JC moved to become an internal auditor for a German cookware company—reviewing the numbers JC saw that the best rewards lay in sales and he resolved to make the unconventional move from auditing into sales. JC threw himself into learning the art of sales, attending many international courses, and reading everything he could. The re-education paid off and he developed an aptitude for sales, rapidly becoming his company's highest achieving salesman. He so impressed the company that he was given a regional position to work in Hong Kong, Taiwan, and Singapore.

But JC wanted to go it alone. His first major entrepreneurial breakthrough came when he was negotiated control of the sales territory of China with a European kitchenware product company. China was a new market for the firm in question and there was much uncertainty about getting into the region. However, over a period of more than 10 years, JC built a sales team of over 500 individuals, achieving 30%-50% sales growth year-on-year.

Today, JC is the founder and director of Li Rong Trading Co which specializes in the distribution of Italian/French and Chinese fashion labels in China. In addition he is a founder and director of Coverstory Specialty Clothing Co Ltd, which specializes in made-to-order uniforms for banks, hotels, airlines, and factories.

JC's business interests keep him on the move around Asia, however, his interest for people development has also resulted in an investment in a leadership development company which organizes training courses for groups of 50 to 1000 people.

JC regularly gives personal development presentations and motivational talks in Chinese and English across Asia.

JC lives in Shanghai with his wife and 2 children.

Grace Liu

Grace Liu is the co-founder of Asianera, a company which specializes in fine hand-painted bone china porcelain with a unique contemporary Asian design aesthetic.

Grace is an American-born Chinese entrepreneur with a passion for ceramics and other traditional hand-crafted arts. Before starting Asianera 14 years ago, Grace worked for IBM's sales and marketing division in New York and Hong Kong.

Having regretfully rebelled against her parents' wishes to learn Chinese, Grace took a year off between high school and university to study Chinese at first-hand in Beijing. This China experience planted the seeds of her desire to discover and understand more about her ancestral motherland. She returned to the US to major in Asian Studies at the University of Michigan, but it wasn't until 1994 that she finally found her way back to China.

Although Grace's passion was for ceramic art, Asianera started as a very small company sourcing Chinese folk art and antique hand-knotted rugs. She had been working in Hong Kong at IBM for several years but felt that the exciting developments happening in China were just out of reach. By starting her own company she was able to combine her artistic interests and fulfill her dream to return to China to be a part of its dynamic development.

It took a while for the company to move from folk art to include ceramics in its range of products. From sourcing ceramics, the company moved into hand-painted artwork, and then manufacturing.

Asianera is committed to maintaining a solid reputation based on high-quality porcelain and innovative design in the country where porcelain was originally invented thousands of years ago. Asianera's fine china is sold globally to exclusive stores, and luxury hotels and restaurants. Under Grace's direction, Asianera sponsors a voluntary program in which the entire company supports the maintenance of a rural elementary school in Hebei province

In recognition of her achievements, Grace received the prestigious 2006 Businesswoman of the Year Award from the Expatriate Professional Women's Society in Shanghai.

She currently lives in Shanghai with her wonderfully supportive husband, and when she's not working she would rather be reading, painting, or getting back to throwing pottery.

Montgomery Singman

Montgomery Singman is the founder and CEO of Radiance Digital Entertainment (radiance.cn), a Shanghai-based online game producer and publisher which is one of the leading pioneers in the online gaming industry. Radiance Digital Entertainment has produced artwork and online games for many companies including Google and Baidu. Their latest titles include Beach Volleyball (radiance.cn/zhuanqu_BeachVollyball_eng.html) and Go Go Racing (radiance.cn/zhuanqu_gogo_eng.html).

Monte was born in Taipei, Taiwan in 1967. His American father went to Taipei to learn Chinese and to search for himself with the 60s hippie crowd. While there he met Monte's mother, and they married. Monte is a CBA (China-born American) but he went to Chinese schools in Taiwan—all the way through to university—so his educational background is 100% Chinese.

At the age of 13, as video arcade games became popular around the world, Taiwan also became the manufacturing center for arcade motherboards, and coin-operated arcade games were everywhere in Taiwan. Monte grew up with Ping Pong, space-invaders, Pac-man and street fighters. At the age of 15, he decided he wanted to make video games. As a result, Monte took computer science as his major so that he had what it took to make video games. Back then, most of the games were created by an army of one-man development companies, and Monte was one of them.

In 1986, at the age of 19, he got his first software published in Taiwan—it was an immediate hit, selling over ten thousand copies. He designed the concept, wrote the program code, designed all the art, wrote the user manual, and even designed the cover. Then he had to convince the software pirates to sell his legitimate software. Within the next two years, Monte published a total of six software packages.

In 1987, Monte read the book "Silicon Valley Fever" and realized the best video gaming talents were in Silicon Valley. Immediately, it was his dream to pack up and go to Silicon Valley to work among some of the best minds in the entertainment software industry. This dream was realized in 1989, when he was 22.

With 1,500 bucks in his pocket, he saw how expensive things were in Silicon Valley. While he sent out resumes to major game companies like Broderbund and Electronic Arts, he worked as a laborer moving boxes in San Francisco dock and pulling out weeds in people's backyards. Fortunately that only lasted for one month before he could find a programmer job.

Monte is now widely considered a veteran of the US video game industry, having participated in the production of hugely successful titles such as John Madden Football, Test

Drive Off-Road series, Street Fighter series, Looney Tunes Racing, Hello Kitty Cubi-land and many others.

He founded and was CEO of Zona which grew to be a leading middleware company. The company was acquired by Shanda Entertainment in 2003 and Monte stayed, managing Shanda's 400 person research and development department until the entrepreneurial calling brought him back to China.

In addition, Monte is the Chief Professor at Shanghai Theater Academy, heading the digital entertainment school and is the author of several books in Chinese on the subject of creativity and next generation online gaming. He is also the founder and main coordinator of International Game Developer Association Shanghai chapter, the most influential trade association for game industry in China.

Richard Robinson

Richard is the CEO and co-founder of Kooky Panda, a venture-backed company creating casual Flash Lite mobile games in their secret labs in Beijing.

Richard grew up in the Boston area where his earliest memories are working in the diner/donut shop his Dad owned. His grandfather and uncles also ran their own food businesses and growing up Richard's Dad would always tell him that his family is from a long line of entrepreneurs all the way back to the "Juneflower" because his Irish ancestors missed the Mayflower.

After high school, Richard took his Boston accent and restaurant skills to the warmer climes of Los Angeles where he worked his way through the University of Southern California as a cook.

While completing an exchange program at Cambridge University in the UK, Richard got the travel bug. Making a deal with his parents that he would work his way around the world as long as he continued to pay his student loans, he hit the road for nearly three years. After stints as a bartender in the Virgin Islands, a concierge in a Swiss Hotel, an English teacher in post-revolution Prague, a house painter in a Norwegian fishing village, a grape picker in France, and an assembly line worker at the BMW Factory in Munich, Richard went overland by train through Siberia and Mongolia on to China, and instantly fell in love with the Middle Kingdom.

Richard then attended an international MBA program at Erasmus University in the Netherlands and while there had his second epiphany when he first surfed the web in 1994.

After graduating, Richard completed a solo 4,000 kilometer bike trip through Africa and then moved to Hong Kong in 1996 to put together his love of China and the internet. Riding the swelling dot com wave he became a founding executive in the internet community startup company renren.com which raised tens of millions of dollars, listed on the Hong Kong Stock Exchange, and was then acquired.

Richard had moved up to Beijing in 2000 with the company and, like many a dot com refugee after the bust, he jumped into the wireless services industry founding a company called MIG that made games for mobile phones. MIG was ultimately acquired by NASDAQ listed Glu Mobile, but Richard remains in Beijing as an active entrepreneur, advisor and angel investor.

As a labor of love on the side, for the past ten years Richard has been running a pan-Asian stand-up comedy club called ChopSchticks which arranges Asian performances of the best US and European comedians. He is a devoted marathon runner and his goal is to run a marathon on every continent by the time he's 45. Richard has two wonderful young sons and is married to a feisty Beijinger. They live on a horse ranch outside of Beijing in a Chinese style courtyard home they built themselves.

Paul Stepanek

Paul Stepanek is the founder of USActive (us-active.com), a company that helps financial institutions and manufacturing companies in China by guiding them through the complex business environment.

Paul was born in Milwaukee, in the US Mid-West, the youngest of seven kids. From an early age he demonstrated his entrepreneurial potential with lemonade stands, yard care services, and house painting. His first lesson in "costs" came early. He was busy counting the day's takings from his street side lemonade stand when his elder sister asked, "How much are you going to pay Mom?"

At first, a bewildered 4-year-old did not understand the question. How could it be possible that anyone else should get any part of this hard earned pile? The gentle explanation that the paper cups and lemonade mix were from the kitchen and that they got there because mom bought them and put them there gave Paul the impetus to cut his mother in on the action.

Paul trained as an industrial engineer at the University of Arizona. After university he went to Taiwan to learn the language and got into manufacturing when he worked for a Taiwanese company as the interface with customers. This experience gave him a great understanding of how product flows through a company and through a manufacturing facility, and he got to see at first hand the troubles that can arise and what customers are expecting to see.

Subsequently Paul went to the US and looked around the Mid-West for a company to hire him to set up a factory for them in China. The confidence and commitment of the young man (he was still in his mid 20s) paid off and through a friend he found a Milwaukee-based company that wanted its production relocated to southern China. Within months he was setting up the equipment and putting the factory together in China.

The company manufactured stamped metal parts that went inside a video cassette: this part was one of the highest volume stamped metal parts in the world with the company making one billion units per year. Paul arrived in China just as video cassette production was migrating from the USA, Japan, and Europe to China.

By 2000 Paul had considerable experience of manufacturing in China and decided to set up USActive so that he could use this experience to add value for organizations that wanted to set up in China. The business started in a very modest way: an idea was pitched to the person who was to become the first client with a laptop while sitting on a sofa. Luckily for the self-financed business, the client agreed, and agreed to pay up front.

USActive now provides due diligence and manufacturing consulting services including market studies, audits, sourcing, QA, facility set-up, import and export, warehousing and local distribution. The company has a team of 35 experienced professionals based in Shanghai and logistics partners based around the world.

Paul enjoys the outdoors and also owns **BOHDI®** ADVENTURES (bohdi.com.cn), a company that provides adventure holidays and manages team building events in China. He is a regular commentator on international business activity in China and frequently provides expert opinion on China in the international media.

Paul lives in Shanghai with his wife Rachel.

Henry Winter

Deng Xiaoping, who led China through reform and dramatically improved the lives of a billion people, once said 实践是检验真理的唯一标准 (facts are the only measure of truth). Henry Winter, who has led a great life in China and dramatically improved the lives of at least a few people, once said 快乐是人生成功的唯一标准 (happiness is the only measure of success).

Henry Winter is the founder and CEO/Chairman of SmartClub Loyalty Management, China's first and largest loyalty points program. He grew up in East Lansing, Michigan and studied French and Finance at the University of Pennsylvania (Wharton).

At school he discovered his natural interest in, and passion for, learning foreign languages. His first "real" job was at Banque Indosuez in France, trading and marketing options and futures. At a "career-advice" Saturday lunch in Paris, two other traders suggested that Henry get an MBA before devoting himself to trading forever. After thinking things over for several hours, Henry decided to quit trading, go back to the US for an MBA, and then move to Taiwan for the immediate following six months to start learning Chinese. He bought his first Mandarin study book on Sunday morning. Four years later, Henry had three Masters degrees: two from Wharton MBA's Lauder Chinese program, and one from Columbia University's School of International Affairs.

After Wharton, Henry worked as a management consultant for Booz Allen Hamilton in Hong Kong, where he became fluent in Cantonese. At that time, his goal was to work in the music business, but each time he interviewed for the desired senior positions, companies kept insisting on "hands-on experience". In January 1998, Henry "jumped into the water" and became an entrepreneur, starting his own "music marketing" company. His theory was that even if the whole thing crashed and burned in six months, at least he would have "experience"!

This led to Groove Street, a company that was founded by Henry who was also the CEO. Groove Street was an interactive marketing agency based in Shanghai which was a pioneer in combining online and offline marketing, and created China's first ever SMS (text) marketing campaign. Groove Street won major regional industry awards in 2001 and 2002, the first mainland China interactive agency to do so. After 2002, the management team of Groove Street decided to focus its energy on developing a scalable business model. Groove Street was sold to an international agency and Smart Club was born.

Today, Henry is a leading expert in online marketing, virtual currencies, and member communities in China. As CEO/Chairman of SmartClub Loyalty Management, he has led China's first loyalty points program to become its largest, with over 2,000,000 Chinese white-collar members. The company has created many innovative programs, which have been studied and copied by leading loyalty programs around the world.

A frequent speaker at national and regional conferences, Henry has been quoted in many international publications. In December 2006, Henry was selected as one of Shanghai's Ten New IT Stars, the first foreigner to even be nominated for this honor.

Henry was also the only foreigner to compete in "Win In China", China's leading business reality game show. Based loosely on The Apprentice, Win In China airs every week on a national channel to an audience of 20,000,000 people. In Season 3, Henry finished 10th out of 150,000 contestants. During one show Henry proposed to his now wife on national television, the first proposal ever on Chinese TV, thereby permanently raising the bar for all Chinese bachelors.

After a grueling day of telling other people what to do, Henry enjoys recovering with a glass of red wine and a foot massage, while watching Star Trek in his home theatre. He is a firm believer in enjoying each day, and pursuing passions now rather than later. After all, if aliens blow up the Earth tonight, what was the point of sacrificing everything for tomorrow?

www.ingramcontent.com/pod-product-compliance
Lightning Source LLC
Chambersburg PA
CBHW060543200326
41521CB00007B/463